For Veronica and Judy

*Life's greatest
treasures shine through
sober eyes*

These days the only bar I ever see
Has got lettuce and tomatoes

Contents

Preface

The Eleventh Tradition of Alcoholics Anonymous states: "Our public relations policy is based on attraction rather than promotion; we need always maintain personal anonymity at the level of press, radio and films." Out of respect for that tradition, many of the participants asked that any reference to Alcoholics Anonymous or AA be deleted from our conversations and replaced with a similar meaning.

Alcoholics Anonymous is responsible for transforming the lives of millions of alcoholics throughout the world. Virtually everyone in the program welcomes the opportunity to express gratitude for its steps, promises and spiritual awakenings. However, many people in *Playing It Straight* who frequent AA meetings and attribute their successful recovery to the Twelve Steps of Alcoholics Anonymous are unable to mention it by name.

Keep in mind, though, that the most successful 12-Step program for recovering alcoholics is Alcoholics Anonymous, which offers a way of life that many in these pages are extremely grateful to have discovered.

Playing It Straight will respect the Eleventh Tradition. I do not wish to offend or upset anyone involved in a recovery program or in the offices of Alcoholics Anonymous by mentioning AA by name.

Acknowledgments

Wherein you compile a project of this magnitude, there are so many people that lend a hand to achieve the final outcome. From the people in these pages to the secretaries who have personally slipped these stars a note praising the book after their agents turned down my initial offer, I thank you.

My sincere gratitude and heartfelt thanks goes to all the participants in the book. The 28 of you changed my life by offering your honesty, gratitude and love throughout these pages. When I met with you, your sole intention was to help others. You have no idea how powerful an impact you have on these readers. Thank you so much for your time, your energy and your participation. I will never forget you or forget our wonderful conversations. My heart is filled with gratitude when I think of our talks, of your sole desire to open up and share your story with the intention of helping others. Thank you all so very, very much. Many of you I have seen since our interview and on a personal note, thank you for your care, your conversations and your friendship.

Many thanks to all of the agents, publicists and managers who took the time to set up the interviews. Some of them were easy to arrange, others took several attempts at coordinating schedules. Hats off to Julie Marvel, Kathy Newman, Sharon McGinley, Keith Garde, Kirk Paskal, Michele Schweitzer, Edna Farley, Douglas Urbanski, Bill Pace, Arielle Ford, Robin Berg, Jon Landau and everyone else in the picture.

Thank you to everyone who helped and supported this project along the way, and especially to my friends and family whose support has been immense. Thank you Steve Lombard, Luther Gillispie, Ralph Grzecki, Lori Norton, Linda Dominick-Lynch, Pat Piligian, Lynn Brophy, Shawn Freeman, Geoffrey Fieger, Les Brown, Brian Tracy, Cindy

Redmond, Pat Collins, Jeff Shoemaker, Donna Salizar, Denise Brown, Haig Avedisian, C. J. Carter, Frank Levy, Mike Beeson, Frederick Courtright, John Morris and everyone else who I may have forgotten. You know who you are. Thank you.

Many thanks to everyone at Health Communications, you have made this a wonderful experience. Thank you Gary Seidler for your initial enthusiasm for the book. Your phone calls were filled with excitement and promise. I appreciate your support. Thank you Peter Vegso for your smooth negotiations throughout the process, and for supporting not only this book but also my upcoming *Playing It Straight* projects plus my second release. Thank you Christine Belleris, who not only put up with my last minute changes but accepted my last second additions with a smile on her face. Thank you Matthew Diener for your meticulous editing and your support of the message contained within these pages. It has been a pleasure. Thank you Kim Weiss and Randee Goldsmith for supporting and promoting this book with everything you've got. Thanks to Lawna Patterson Oldfield for designing a terrific looking cover, and to the entire art department for making the book look sharp, inside and out. Can't wait for the next one!

Many thanks to my mother who has endured the good with the bad (mostly bad if you include my teenage years). Our relationship has blossomed into a beautiful one, filled with gratitude, love and joy. Thank you for being there when I needed you. I love you Mom.

Thank you to my wife, Judy, whose support has been continuous throughout this project. She has been a fixture of inspiration and has assisted me in every facet of this project. She's held my hand during the difficult times and hugged me during the joyful times. Thank you for everything Judy. I love you darling.

And to my five-year-old bundle of joy, Veronica, who, without knowing it, has been my single greatest inspiration in life and for this book. Many times late at night when I was working, I opened your door and kissed you on the cheek, then looked at you as you slept, tears filling my eyes with joy. You have made me discover the true love in my heart. Thank you for just being you.

Many thanks also to the artists who let me use their work as quotes and chapter titles.

And thank you Steven Tyler. Our 90-minute conversation changed my life. You were just doing what you were supposed to do, just helping another alcoholic see the light. Your words and genuine care gave me the initial force to move out of the dark and welcome the light. Not a day goes by when I don't think of you and of our conversations. Thank you Steven, thank you for lifting me up and assisting me with my first steps on the greatest, most spectacular journey of my life.

Introduction

I remember the moment as if I were still in it. My hands were trembling, voice cracking. My throat was dry. My thoughts were precisely focused on the one specific question that I was aching to have answered. The moment was 20 minutes overdue. The phone call should have come by now. My mind was thriving with deception and disbelief. I sat firmly in my chair, eyes glued to the telephone.

With the power of an ear-piercing shriek, the phone rang. My heart stood still. I grabbed it on the second ring. I needed to know the answer to that one burning question.

This was my fourth attempt at interviewing Steven Tyler, Aerosmith's animated troubadour. For the previous three bids, I was the music critic for two Michigan newspapers. Although his publicists would never admit it, my circulation wasn't large enough to deserve an audience with rock's original bad boy.

This time, though, I had my ammo: a weekly column distributed by the Los Angeles Times Syndicate. I was national. Steven Tyler's publicists agreed to an interview. But this time, unlike the previous hat tricks of attempts over the last five years, his music and the band's latest album, *Pump,* were the furthest things from my mind. Steven Tyler didn't know it, but he was about to change my life.

My deadline was less than four hours away. It was business as usual according to my editor. I was to finish the phone interview and write the story. I had a concert to review that night.

"David Dodd, how are you?" Tyler asked in a friendly voice.

"Good, Steven, good," I replied with a subtle uncertainty. "Steven . . . ," I said, then paused.

I was always sharp during interviews. Always on top of the situation. I continually struck up interesting and exciting conversations. Not this time. My emotions were on overload.

"Sobriety and success, what a combination," I blurted out.

"No shit," he replied.

My heart was pounding through my chest. I was sweating. I needed his help. Tyler had been sober for quite some time. I desperately wanted a piece of that. I urgently needed to know his secret. *How did he do it?* That was the question leaping for attention.

I figured if Tyler could quit, then some way, somehow, maybe he could give me the secret to end my battle with alcohol. My addiction was killing me, killing my relationships and killing every one of the goals I set. I was crashing and burning. I never would admit that to anyone. Not until this very moment.

"My God, I've been sober for three days," I said, immediately feeling the relief. "Help me, Steven. I need help."

It was the first step at jumping out of my denial. The first shine of a transformation.

"Are you serious?" he asked.

"Very serious," I replied, as the second wave of relief sprang from my shoulders.

"Well, good fucking for you, man," Tyler announced with joy.

My emotions were rocking. I went from complete desperation and fear to astonishing relief. Once again, my emotional roller coaster was soaring.

"Are you really serious about this?" Tyler asked again.

"Very serious."

"Do you want to learn something that you'll wish on everybody because it's such an amazing secret, and it's so simple?" he continued. "Go to 90 meetings in 90 days. Do the 90/90.

"I fought it for five years. When they tell you to do the 90/90, there's something in that. You'll get it in the first 90 days. It's a real spiritual, cleansing, people-oriented trip that is second to none. There's nothing else on this planet that is as rewarding and cleansing and filled with joyful bliss. You'll meet super friends and you'll walk around higher than you ever got on any drug."

We spent the next 25 minutes talking about the fears and denial of the disease, the co-dependency issues and the rewards of recovery. Tears were flowing down my face. This was the guy I'd admired all through my high school days. The person that I always wanted to meet and interview, to party and hang out with. Those desires never came to pass, but when I needed his influence to begin my transformation, he was there. Steven Tyler was there for me. That blew me away.

Before we hung up, Tyler gave me the pseudonym he uses on the road when he checks into hotels and told me where he'd be staying in Detroit the following week. He set me up with four tickets and backstage passes, and said he'd like to spend some time with me while he was in town.

How's that for follow-up? I couldn't believe it.

I was riding on top of the world that week. Hitting as many meetings as I could, trying to absorb the steps. There was a lot to learn. Mostly, there was a lot of my old behavior that I had to *unlearn*.

The night of the show, three friends and I had great seats at Pine Knob and watched a sizzling set that hot August night. I couldn't concentrate on the songs; my mind was racing, wondering if Tyler would remember me. I knew he talked with hundreds of people each week. I was hoping that we'd be able to spend some time together. Looking back, there was a vital part of my sobriety that I didn't have back then—I didn't *believe*. I should have known that everything would work out just fine.

We were ushered into a room filled with 70 or 80 people, all eagerly waiting to meet the band. Fifteen minutes later, Joey Kramer, Brad Whitford and Tom Hamilton arrived with Perriers in their hands. They were immediately surrounded. Several minutes passed, but still no sign of Tyler. Eager eyes fell upon Joe Perry as he walked in a few minutes later. I was getting nervous. I found a couple guys on the crew and told them I was a friend of Tyler's, that he wanted to get together with me after the show. They told me he had already left.

I quickly made my way to the parking lot behind the amphitheater, where the tour buses were parked. The rest of the band was headed in that direction, too. Within moments there were several hundred people swarming the parking lot.

Four bodyguards headed toward the door of the theater. They were keeping the crowd clear of their prize possession: Steven Tyler. I was 50 feet away from them and knew I had no chance of closing the distance because of the human bottleneck between us.

I cupped my hands around my mouth and yelled, "Hey, Steven, I'm David Dodd!" And just like in the movies, he stopped. The four guys surrounding him came to a sudden halt. "Over here!" I yelled, raising my hands in the air. I couldn't believe what was happening. "Wait a minute," Tyler said. "I want to talk to this guy."

One of the bodyguards motioned for me to join them. Instantly my friends and I were whisked inside while the other fans watched in amazement. Once inside, Tyler greeted me with a big hug. "How you doing?" he asked with a big smile. "Let's go where we can talk." We sat and talked on the Pine Knob stage for nearly an hour. It was an amazing night, an incredible time for me.

I couldn't believe that he would spend his time with me, with someone he didn't know, but Steven Tyler wanted to help me. He wanted me to be sober, to regain my strength and my sanity. His actions were the firm foundation I needed to begin this journey of transformation.

I will always be grateful for his words, his kindness and his genuine care. That night still blows me away.

Back in the Saddle

It has taken some time for this collection to reach you. Some of these interviews have been preserved for a couple years, others are fresh. Nonetheless, the message is strong and effective. Many people have given me their time and honesty to pass on the secrets and success of their personal recovery. I am very grateful to each and every one of them.

We all experience pain and tears, hope and joy, fear and lack of self-esteem. We are all woven from the same thread. I learned a tremendous amount from these brothers and sisters. They welcomed me into their homes for honest and insightful conversations. This book has been a spiritual awakening for me.

Recovery is serious business. It continues to be the most difficult effort of my life. However, the more I live the steps in my everyday life and conform to the principles I've been taught, the easier it flows, the greater the rewards. I won't kid you: the beginning was an agonizing, brutal task. It wasn't easy for me.

Although many people close their eyes to the vision, the truth is that alcohol and drug abuse run rampant in our society. Many people in this book are on the front lines; they work in treatment centers, counsel people, hit meetings several times a week. We all have reached the same conclusion: the alcohol and drug epidemic has not declined, not in the least bit.

Just look at the facts.

Forty percent of male high school seniors get drunk on a regular basis. Americans *under* 21 drink more than one billion cans of beer a year. The National Council of Alcoholism says that 30 percent of the nation's nine-year-olds feel the pressure to drink. Nine-year-olds!

Eighty-eight percent of high school coaches surveyed said that alcohol poses the greatest threat to high school athletes. More than half of all teenage fatalities are alcohol-related. Imagine a jumbo jet crashing with no survivors—three times a week. That is the number of Americans killed in accidents involving drunk drivers—70 a day, 26,000 annually. Additionally, more than 1.5 million are injured.

At least 22 million Americans have a serious alcohol problem. Eight million are teenagers. Many of those interviewed in this book, including me, believe these figures are very conservative. The fact is, hundreds of thousands die each year from alcohol-related accidents and health problems. On an average Friday or Saturday night, 1 out of every 10 drivers on the road is drunk: think about that when you're on the road this weekend.

We live in a society that accepts drunken behavior. People use the excuse of being drunk for their inexcusable acts. "Why did you do that?" "Oh, I was drunk." How many times have you heard that? They address it as if it was an excusable situation. "I'm sorry I said that or I did that, but you know, I was drunk." And the other person supports it, "That's all right, I know what you mean."

How many fights and arguments have you seen in bars and clubs late at night? Problems arise on nearly every occasion when you have a gathering of people drinking—sporting events, concerts: the list is long. It's the alcohol talking.

People don't get behind the wheel with the intention of getting in a car accident or killing someone. When alcohol is in their system, the trouble begins. Why are so many people late for work on Mondays? Because they have a hangover. Statistics show that there is one day of the year when more people report to work late or miss the entire day altogether: the day after the Super Bowl. All because they have alcohol in their system.

We need to banish the excuses; to abolish the justification of everyone allowing this behavior to continue. I said it before: 1 out of every 10 people on the road on weekend nights are operating a vehicle under the influence. One out of every 10. They say it's okay, they've just had a little to drink. Maybe they're a little drunk but that's acceptable to them. When their judgment is all messed up and they cross the yellow line and hit a minivan head on, it's not okay. They've just shattered the lives of an entire family.

The excuse for being drunk is a bunch of baloney. We need to eliminate the word "drunk" from our vocabulary. These people are completely wasted, that's what they are.

If someone can't walk a straight line, can't see straight, can't hold an intelligent conversation and continues to feed his body alcoholic toxins, that person's thinking is completely wasted. They are wasting their lives, wasting their time, wasting the lives of their loved ones. They're just wasting away.

A judge will call it driving under the influence. A friend will call it being drunk. I call it wasted. Let's get out of the enabling here and call it what it is. Look a person straight in the eyes the next time he's drunk. Or if it's you, take a good, honest look in the mirror. What do you see? You see a person who's completely wasted. That's what you see. Don't give me any of this cute conversation about being drunk. You know what you are.

I don't mean to sound angry here. My intention is not to relate with you in that manner, but how else can I put it? I can say people get drunk or intoxicated, but then I'd be supporting their conduct as many others do. I've seen so much of this crazy behavior that I'm no longer able to shadow it under a sugar coating that hides the poison pill it truly is. Accepting this behavior is ridiculous.

Don't forget that I was on the other end of this equation. I was the one whose life was wasting away. Maybe that's why I take such a firm stand on the excuses—I mastered them. Think about it. Being able to use the word "drunk" is one of the greatest crutches a drinker has because it's so acceptable in our society. The behavior of a practicing alcoholic is not acceptable.

It was acceptable for Nirvana's Kurt Cobain to use heroin. I heard him talk about it on numerous occasions during interviews. Several journalists have pointed it out in their articles. A few weeks before his death he was rushed to the hospital because of an OD. He made it sound so glamorous. It wasn't glamorous when Cobain blew his brains out. He was alone in his house. He died alone.

A few years back, Def Leppard guitarist Steve Clark died because he overloaded his body with toxins. The coroner's report stated that

Clark died of a fatal mixture of alcohol and drugs. The alcohol level in his blood was three times the British legal limit for driving. The autopsy revealed traces of Valium and morphine along with a fatal quantity of codeine. He was taking painkillers as a result of a back injury. Clark's body virtually shut down because it couldn't digest any additional chemicals or liquid toxins. He was feeding his body poisons quicker than it could process all of them, so his brain told the rest of his body to shut down.

The celebrities continue to die: Brian Jones, Jim Morrison, Jimi Hendrix, Janis Joplin. AC/DC's Bon Scott died of acute alcohol poisoning; Dennis Wilson drowned while intoxicated; Thin Lizzy's Phil Lynott, John Belushi, Sid Vicious, River Phoenix, John Bonham, Keith Moon, they all died of abusing alcohol and drugs. Blind Melon vocalist Shannon Hoon recently died of a drug overdose. He was found in the back of his tour bus at 1:20 in the afternoon, just hours before a scheduled concert. The band had a successful debut album and had just released their highly anticipated sophomore disc. They planned on supporting the work with an 18-month tour. He had all the success he needed, and a beautiful 4-year-old daughter. His manager had put him into rehab twice, but Shannon Hoon made the mistake of not realizing how deadly this disease is.

It's sad because these were all good people. Good people who died because of a disease they couldn't control.

Sweet Emotion

Steven Tyler gave me a tremendous gift. His attention brought many of my emotions to the surface. It was the beginning of a great self-realization. That's one of the gifts that recovery has given me—a grand awareness of my emotions. I am now able to touch, feel, smell, listen and relish the joys of life. Before my recovery program, I was teeming with a negativity that hampered my dreams and goals. I was still very active in my writing career, still achieved the highest level possible without realizing how greatly alcoholism limited my potential. It put a complete halt to my achievements. Although I wouldn't admit it, I was miserable. I wanted to escape reality, wanted no responsibility. That was my denial. I didn't know that. I was unaware of life's immense rewards, oblivious to the great bliss that surrounded me.

During the last few months of my drinking, I had a friend who often asked, "David, who's your worst enemy?" I kept mentioning a couple people I didn't get along with, kept trying to think of who she was talking about. Even though she kept telling me, I never fully realized that my own greatest enemy was me.

I was fortunate to have been given a second chance. Many others have not been so lucky. I was given the opportunity to regain my spirit. Somewhere inside, your spirit is watching you. Mine was buried under layers of negativity, self-doubt and anger. Now it flourishes with daily miracles.

I am ready and open to accept these miracles. I have the intent. There are people who say miracles never happen to them; they don't believe in them. Yet the people who believe, those who truly believe they are intended for a miracle, continue to live these miracles on a regular basis. They may not be these elaborate, earth-shattering miracles you hear about on television, but these small, very significant occurrences are still miracles.

Let's not lose sight of who we truly are. Each and every one of us intends to move forward with great success. Many times, however, we lose that focus.

Many people are comfortable with being mediocre. For some, an average student holding onto a C grade is acceptable. Average is acceptable. In many cases, students and parents alike are overjoyed that the kids didn't get a D. Just making it through the school year with an average grade is acceptable to many people.

I spend a lot of time with successful people who can't even imagine being mediocre. It simply is not a way of life for them.

I used to have a 50-minute ride to work in the morning and another 45-minute ride going home. In my last couple years at that job, instead of listening to morning radio and switching the channels constantly, I'd listen to motivational tapes. It really changed the way I focused on my day. I now welcome the opportunity of success. When I listen to Earnie Larsen, Les Brown, Tony Robbins, Father Leo, Wayne Dyer or countless others, they uplift my spirit at six in the morning. You can't help but be motivated when you listen to these guys. Now I can't wait to get in the car and listen to a tape. I'm almost a fanatic about it. Instead of getting excited about the new Pearl Jam release, I call the bookstores to see when Deepak Chopra's new tape will be released. Crazy at times, but it's amazing how it works for me.

Still, there are countless others who wallow in mediocrity. I remember walking to school in the fifth grade. I would pass a giant pond next to our school and look through the wire fence surrounding it. In the far corner was this slimy green scum collecting on the surface. Every day it would be there looking the same: no change, no movement, nothing at all. That's what happens to people who accept mediocrity in their lives—they become pond scum. It's that simple. Look at the comparisons: many people are happy with just a passing grade, whether in school, at work or in relationships. People accept mediocrity on a daily basis. Just as I don't accept the word "drunk" in our vocabulary, "mediocrity" should be replaced with "pond scum."

There are many things that get in the way of success, but they only get there if we let them. We each have a distinct personality, a solitary spirit that needs to emerge. This book is filled with many remarkable spirits. All the participants agreed to these interviews with the sole intention of helping others who currently share or have shared the same experiences, both before and after sobriety. You will learn some tremendous lessons from these people.

I still go back and read certain interviews over and over. It gives me strength. These are the voices of people who have been there for me. They've given me significant advice and powerful thoughts. Now they're here for you.

Enjoy this collection, and if you ever run into one of the people on these pages, don't forget to thank them.

Chapter 1

THE BEGINNING

We're seeing things in a different way
and God knows it ain't his.

—Aerosmith
"Livin' on the Edge"

Anthony Kiedis

Anthony Kiedis is a recovering alcoholic and drug addict. He's the lead singer and lyricist for The Red Hot Chili Peppers.

I suffered a great deal because not only did I take on my dad's drug-using tendencies at a very early age, but in the long run the whole lifestyle accelerated my addiction.

I moved from Michigan to California when I was 11. I didn't know my father personally because my parents split up when I was one. He came out to Hollywood and my mother stayed in Michigan. I knew I wanted to be just like him, even though I didn't know what he was like.

So when I was 11, I told my mom that I was going to live with my dad. I have a tremendous amount of respect and love for him today, but when I was 11 years old, he was kind of the ultimate Hollywood scenester, playboy, wanna-be gangster, legend-in-his-own-mind type of character. To me he seemed like the greatest thing in the world. He was very

3

intelligent, warm, loving—thought I was the greatest thing in the world—but was very much caught up in the whole flurry of drug use and irresponsibility. He had a lot of pluses and a lot of minuses.

When I was a kid I used to think, *This is the greatest in the world. My friends have parents that work all day long, they don't have any kind of sincere relationship, and my dad's the coolest.* But in actuality I suffered a great deal because not only did I take on his drug-using tendencies at a very early age, but in the long run the whole lifestyle accelerated my addiction.

We established a relationship as friends—almost like brothers rather than father and son—because I was a very mature young man. I found myself taking on the responsibility of making sure he was going to be okay. I didn't want him to die. I didn't want him to get too loaded and go out and get beat up because he became belligerent. There was a daily anxiety that I had of making sure that Pops was going to be okay because I loved the guy so much. I didn't want to see anything bad happen to him. We went through a lot of terrible times.

When I was 15, a sophomore in high school, I had just come home from school one day around three o'clock. Dad was involved with some illegal transactions involving narcotics. Though he has since had a complete moral revolution, at the time that's how he supported himself in several different ways, financially and drug-wise. I came home and put my books down on the table and my dad ran into the living room. He looked out the window and he froze. I was like, "What's up, Dad?" and he went, "See those guys coming up the side-walk? See those guys coming?" I said, "Yeah, what about them?" He said, "Those guys are undercover cops." There were five or six of them dressed in street clothes. We just stood there in the living room. We both knew he had a lot of things in the closet he could be arrested for. Then two or three of them smashed through the front door just like *kaboom,* straight down, big wooden door. Some guys were coming in the back door, others through the windows. Me and my dad were basically stuck there with a bunch of shotguns pointing at us.

They handcuffed us together, sat us on the couch and ransacked the house. They found the goods in the closet and took my father away to jail. One more time I'm sitting there in my house going, *How am I going to get him out of this mess?*

I got somebody to put up their house for bail. We spent all of the money that we'd saved on a lawyer to get my dad out of this mess;

thank God we did because I wanted my dad in the pad. That's when we realized that he could no longer live that way.

He became a struggling actor, and still is. That was the type of environment I was exposed to growing up. It was inevitable I would end up spending my life with drugs. Whatever it is that causes people to have this need—be it a combination of genetics, social surroundings, parental behavior toward them as children—everything leads up to someone needing to hide behind the fix, whether it's alcohol or drugs. The process was accelerated in my case because it was so available. It was weird because my dad kind of steered me away from it just about the time that I dove into it head first. He was scratching his head, wondering why I was living that lifestyle. It was like, *Dad, wake up and smell the slime. I'm an extension of your life.*

Lou Gossett Jr.

Lou Gossett Jr. is a recovering alcoholic and drug addict. He's appeared in numerous motion pictures including *An Officer and a Gentleman,* the role in which he earned an Oscar for Best Supporting Actor.

*I was one of those victims.
I did not know that I had an allergic reaction to it. I ignored it completely.
Thank God I recognized my allergic reaction—the obsession of my mind—in time to say that the buck stops here in my family.*

When I was a kid, I lived in the basement. I didn't have my own bedroom, so me and my cousins were always put in a spare room while our parents partied. We could go and have the food and stuff, but after a while, we were put there to sleep. None of us would go to sleep, though, because there were a lot of great, great sounds like Duke Ellington and Count Basie music on the 78s. People were dancing and laughing. Every now and then there was a fight and the women would be worried, but they loved their husbands so much they took care of them. The one thing I really remember is it smelled like love. That smell of alcohol was like love to me.

Every last man in my family, my father and uncles on both sides, abused themselves one way or another with substance. They were all my heroes. They thought—and this is what I was taught as a kid— you partied on Friday and Saturday nights, and Sunday morning you went to church and you had a quiet Sunday afternoon and evening. Then you were ready to go to work on Monday.

Friday and Saturday nights: that's the reward to the poor—the poor working man, anyway. That was my example of celebration. If you won something, if you succeeded in something, you celebrated. Looking back, I've realized that all the men in my family died of alcoholism.

If alcohol or something didn't work too well in my system, I thought it was an inadequacy because you were supposed to drink. You were supposed to party and stay up all night long and take your woman home and make her feel good, too. That was the man, and I worked and I succeeded in everything I worked hard at; in the business, somewhat in sports—I succeeded in everything I tried. I was definitely going to succeed in being able to handle my alcohol and my marijuana. Cocaine was terrible because it closed my nose in the early days, so I stopped that.

I succeeded in the hash and I was able to have fun and stay up. I forced myself to stay up, whatever I had to do, whatever it took. I took pills to stay up, to prove I was a man. All the time obviously lying to myself because none of it really worked.

I had started to abuse completely when I hit freebase. I used freebase because it got the girls. The girls loved it, they were slaves to it. It brought the macho out in me. All along, what it was doing was hiding the bashfulness and shyness of courtship and the whole thing. I wasn't good at that. A lot of times I didn't get the girl to go to bed, which was the thing to do. With freebase I found an easy way to achieve that.

I believe now, in hindsight, that if you use things like that in an immoral way, to get women or to make slaves of people, it bites you. It bit me because of the reasons I used it—to make love to women, sometimes more than one. The first thing that stopped was my sexual activity. I got soft and flaccid in sex. I became the laughing stock and blamed it on everything. I blamed it on the kind of women. I blamed it on the kind of cocaine. I didn't take enough vitamins. I wasn't eating enough. I went through a whole rationalization.

The drugs worked for a while, but I made them my lord, my God. My work and being a father and being a man—the responsible citizen—was all secondary. I was in love with that feeling. Some of the most beautiful women I've ever seen, I would get them in my home and I'd give them one puff of that stuff and it was over. It was incredible to feel that. Obviously I was hiding a feeling of self-inadequacy all that time.

I pretty much had control of my substance use until I came to California and met a woman who led me into the world of freebase. This was around 1983, 1984, in and around the time of *An Officer and a Gentleman.*

I wasn't feeling the effects of it during the movie. I was at my strongest. I still had the syndrome of Friday and Saturday night, so Monday through Friday I had to work extra hard to get my energy and stuff together. I did my extra pushups. I ran my extra couple of miles. I was in that regimen. I came to the show in excellent shape.

But right after I finished the movie, I went right back to it and it tipped the scale. Freebase made me feel like King Kong. It makes you feel wonderful and it got the girls. I had everything I ever read about in *Penthouse.* But slowly and surely you need more to get that feeling. More and more and more. Crack is even worse because it's dirty and you don't know what else is in it. It's the worst thing there is, makes you a slave immediately.

It stopped working for me during that time, but I couldn't stop. I tried to keep it a secret from everyone. I got real paranoid, had hallucinations. I was in and out of the hospital three or four times, secretly. I managed to do some work, do little bits here and there, but as soon as I had four or five days off, I'd go deeper. I wouldn't sleep, wouldn't eat, the quality of my women was lower and lower. I finally had to pay them, and even then they wouldn't show up.

You rationalize the reasons why it didn't work last time: it was the wrong type of stuff, the wrong time of day, next time you'll eat and then you'll go to the steam room and sweat it out of your body. Then you'll go to work the next day, all of that, all the rationalizations. Takes a while for you to run out of reasons.

I was one of those victims. I did not know that I had this allergic reaction to it. I ignored it completely. Thank God I recognized my allergic reaction—the obsession of my mind—in time to say that the buck stops here in my family. It is a miracle. I did nothing but show up at meetings and do what I was told. For the first time ever, I didn't take over.

Chapter 11

DENIAL

*There's a sadness in your style,
an empty room behind your smile.*

—The Knack
"One Day at a Time"

n a later chapter, Gregory Harrison mentions something very important. "By the time you realize you have a problem," he says, "it's an old problem." Very true for many of us. Drinking is such a popular pastime that the abusing stage is often ignored.

I rarely thought I had a problem because my friends were drinking as much as I was. We went out, we drank, we got drunk. Crazy things happened to us. The escapades continued, both good and bad. We rarely went out to have a drink or two. We'd go out and do it up. Maybe if I had been with people who drank a couple drinks while I plowed through seven or eight, it would have been apparent that my drinking pattern was different. Someone may have even brought it to my attention.

However, alcoholics have an uncanny talent of attracting one another. We support each other's illness. It generally isn't until the drinking problem is placed directly in our face that we address it, and that's the last thing we want to do. That's where denial commands attention. Alcoholism and drug abuse are the only diseases that tell you that you don't have them. King denial.

I was a music critic for quite some time. Backstage at concerts the drinks, and oftentimes drugs, were flowing. I'd go to the local clubs and bartenders would buy me drinks. My job situated me in places that served liquor. My instrument of abuse was readily available. Looking back, I can see I was at the disaster point for the last three or four years of my drinking. My life was falling apart. I lied to my friends, lied to my family and, worst of all, lied to myself. Trying to deceive myself was a continuous calling for me. I constantly cornered myself in lies, then tried to tap dance my way out.

I thought I drank because of the chaos in my life, all the problems with no solutions in sight. Drinking temporarily lifted the craziness. I soon discovered that the problems and the chaos surrounding my life were directly attributed to my drinking and, more directly, my thinking. Drinking was a symptom of my dysfunctional thinking. I didn't realize that. My denial blinders concealed reality.

I promised myself I'd quit. I promised a lot of people. I lied to them again and again. The cunning aspect of this disease is that it makes us do whatever we have to do to keep it going, to continue the pace. I kept trying to make deals with myself: *I'll only have a couple tonight, I won't drive home drunk,* or *I'll only drink at home so I won't be on the road.*

Near the end I was consumed with quitting. I would wake up and promise myself that I wouldn't drink that day. I'd feel incredibly guilty. I thought every time I drank it would be different, hoping the outcome would change. I continued to drink, expecting different results. That's insane. It's ludicrous to conduct the same behavior expecting different results. It just doesn't happen that way.

My disease continued to talk to me, trying to convince me I wasn't sick—I was just going through bad times. *It will change next time,* I thought, *things will be different.* Nothing changed. The guilt was growing, the antics grew worse, the lies deepened. I handed in my work at the very last minute. My editors were frustrated. My mind was cluttered. The liquor flowed; I was fighting to keep the buzz going. All the time, the relics of pain and sorrow were taking their toll.

My life was distorted. The consequences of drinking had done me in. Still, the voice in my head said it would pass. *Maybe I should try a new career,* it said, *or new friends.* I was always blaming others for my own demise. My guilt, meanwhile, was astonishing, overwhelming at times. My emotions were shattered. I didn't know what to do, what to think. Drinking wasn't working for me. It wasn't the answer. Still my denial was winning. Denial was leading my life. I continued to live the style of devastation that I was used to, clinging to my old habits. It nearly killed me.

Tony Sales knows all about denial. Following a terrifying automobile accident, his doctors informed him that even the slightest amount of drugs or alcohol could immediately kill him. "So I rushed to my dealer and bought an ounce of cocaine," he says.

That's how powerful this disease is. Never underestimate the strength of addiction.

Tony Sales

Tony Sales is a recovering alcoholic and drug addict. He's played with a number of bands, including three world tours with Iggy Pop. He's been the bassist for Tin Machine since its inception.

I hear some wonderful things
at meetings that I never heard in my
dealer's home. Humility is not thinking
less of yourself; it's thinking of
yourself less. It keeps me focused.
It's a focus that I need to live with.

I had been up, once again, all night. My brother Hunt and I had just finished a world tour with Iggy. On our time off we put together a 12-piece band with a five-piece horn section and we fronted the band, like a Sam and Dave kind of thing. So on the third night of this gig we were doing at a club in town, I went back to my new apartment. I had just moved in that day, did two shows that night, and then proceeded to stay up all night with the guitar player in the band.

16

At about 5:30 A.M. we decided to go get some more cocaine. We jumped in the car and went up one of the canyons in town. Then we were on the way down, and that's all I remember. Our guitar player told me later that the brakes locked and the car went into a hydroplane. I hit a telephone pole at about 70 miles/hour and he was thrown from the car, his left arm snapped in two.

They found me with the stick shift through my chest and my head was crushed. I was in a coma. I was in surgery for 19 hours. They didn't give me any percentage to live. I was in intensive care for ten days.

I came out of the coma ten days later, and the doctor came in my room and told me I was going to die. I couldn't really think well at that point; I wasn't really in touch with my emotions. I didn't want to die. I looked down at my body: I was covered with stitches. I thought, *I've really done it this time.* I thought I was really in trouble now and at the same time I thought, *Man, I'm chosen. I must have a hot line to God because I'm scot-free here. If I can go through this stuff, obviously I'm meant to keep on going.* The denial was so profound. I was in the hospital recovering from the accident for three months or so, some of which was spent in a wheelchair.

My wife (at the time) slept in the room on a couch, and I had a lot of support from my family and friends. I finally left the hospital, and a couple weeks later I was using and drinking again. That's the denial of this disease. It's the only disease there is that tells you you don't have it. I started drinking and using again until she left, or actually until I booted her out. I mean, sure, she left. I lost everything else that I hadn't lost previously in the accident, and I hit an incomprehensible bottom I saw no way out of.

By this time I had met another woman, whom I'm still with today. She was pregnant and giving birth to my son. I helped deliver the child at home, and, as soon as he was born, I was out looking for drugs at six or seven in the morning. I couldn't stand to feel my feelings. My feelings were my whole life and I didn't know that they were just feelings, that the only truth is actually what I'm saying at the moment. That's what the truth really is for me in my life; it's not what's happening down the line.

I tried to get the big picture and, as far as I'm concerned, the big picture is bullshit. It's the one-day-at-a-time picture, the small increment of time I walk where my life leads me. It's not what I was doing ten years ago, what I'm going to be doing a few months from now; it's right now. When I stay in the present as much as I can, I feel more comfortable. I mean, I always wanted to have control over everything, so finally I put myself in a position where I can have some sort of control of my life if I just stay in the moment and try to stay in solution.

Today what I do is show up no matter what my head tells me because my head doesn't really consider me as a person; my head just considers what it wants. Today, I help other people instead of just helping myself, and it seems to keep me sober and clean. I can't say enough of it. I have a life today rather than just an existence. Anytime I get overwhelmed with whatever's going on, I get to talk to other people about it and share how I feel, which doesn't seem to be much different from how they feel. I'm a man among men today instead of a stranger to my fellow man and to myself. For that, I'm grateful. I'm grateful that I'm alive.

The car accident was no surprise to me, and the fact that I was high was no surprise to me. I wasn't surprised when I'd find myself on the floor in some foreign country retching and thinking, *God, I'm going to stop this. This is the last time I'm going to do this.* I knew all those nights and mornings that I had a problem, but decided that tomorrow was the day I was going to stop.

I felt I had the power to stop myself, on my own. I felt that I had to do it on my own—which itself is a complete ego trip, that we think we have to do it alone, that we have the power to do it alone. Well, tomorrow never came. There was just more heartache in tomorrow.

I had the same experience every day. I was looking for and recovering from. I certainly wasn't taking life as it came and enjoying the moments. I didn't have any moments of peace. I didn't have any moments between my ears; it was all chaos and chaotic every moment. I knew I had a problem, but I just would not face it. I did not want to grow up. I did not want to venture out into my own life. I don't regret anything I might have missed because whatever dues I had to pay to get where I am today, that's what I had to do. I understand that.

Possibly, if someone had come to me earlier in life and pointed out that I was going in the wrong direction, then possibly I would have done something. But self-denial and defiance are characteristics of where we come from, so I don't try to tell anybody how to live their lives. It's just not my business to do that. My business is to just make sure I can support others who want to lead clean and sober lives because I have that experience. It's one day at a time.

We're doing this interview and it's only Friday, so that's the only day I've got: Friday. And keeping it that simple for me was never a priority. I spoke about it before; if I didn't have three or four days of chaos going, I was a loser. It's just not that way now. I know many musicians and entertainers who are not diving into drugs and alcohol for the solution because that's an old script, that live-hard-and-die-young thing. I guess to paraphrase someone I worked with, I've got a lust for life now. That's where I'm coming from.

The substance kept me in bondage in my own head. It held me back from my own life and from growing up, from maturing into a person who could advance into his own life and know there's nothing out there that's gonna kill him just because he takes a chance.

If I show up for a job and I don't get it, I don't care; there's another job. There's no person out there that can take anything away from me; I was doing that myself. It might feel frightening or scary to walk into the dark, but that's where the treasure might lie. The treasure of my own life lies there sometimes. So I take the step, I walk on faith or walk with faith. Where there's faith there's no fear, as I've been told, and I agree. If I'm going to sit in fear I'll just be sitting alone. If I can walk with faith, there are others on that path with me who will help me when I fall and help me up to keep walking. I mean, a moving target is harder to hit, so I just keep going.

I put so much faith in drugs and alcohol before, like they were going to do something for me. All they were doing was killing me. I knew that they were killing me and yet it's not that I couldn't stop; it's that I wouldn't. I had all the information, but information alone could not keep me away from the terminal illness I believe alcoholism is. I had all the information in the world, as a lot of us do. I found out there are no payoffs. Just because I get the right job doesn't mean I'll fix it, or the right car, whatever, money in the bank—it won't do it. It's an inside job. It has to come from within. That's where the peace lies. Even though nothing outside of me can change me, and nothing outside of me can keep me clean and sober, I have to rely on something greater than myself. Even when I don't believe that there is something, I still pretend that I believe and it seems to work. It feels good to be able to go to sleep at night with me and wake up with me and not be afraid to do so. I don't have to wake up with a stranger in bed with me and wonder what I said to her last night or have to return the car that I stole or any of that stuff.

I don't believe I was put on earth for the sole purpose of feeling good and seeing what I could get out of life. I think it's just as possible that I was put here to learn and see what I could give back because for me it is in the giving that I seem to be given. In the seven years I've been sober, I've seen a lot of people come and go and, more often than not, it's those people who do not have faith, who will not try to find some humility—they are the ones who slip.

I hear some wonderful things at meetings that I never heard in my dealer's home. Humility is not thinking less of yourself; it's thinking of yourself less. It keeps me focused. It's a focus that I need to live with. I tried to get that focus through substance and consequently never got any focus at all. I'm still on the path, looking for that focus today, and I'm living a life I'm beginning to enjoy. I didn't particularly think that was possible. I had people tell me that there was another way to live and that I didn't have to feel the way I did any longer if I didn't want to, but I wasn't ready to hear them.

At the end of my using, I didn't have low self-esteem—I had no self-esteem. I went to meetings but walked out of them. There was a bar on the corner near where this one meeting was, and I had them pour me a beer in a plastic cup. I toasted alcohol out of my life and said, *This will be my last drink. Give me the strength to carry on, God.*

I had hit a bottom that I didn't want to ever hit again. I used my depression and my demoralization to spur me on to get clean and sober that day. I just stayed in recovery. I was depressed and I could not live with myself any longer the way I was living, the way that I was existing. It was certain death for me; I started to have seizures after the car accident as a result of doing cocaine and alcohol, and the injuries that I sustained in my head. My neurologist told me that I could die instantly if I did any recreational drugs or drank, so I proceeded to go right to my dealer's house and get an ounce of cocaine.

The denial was there and the information didn't phase me whatsoever. I didn't care about information. I mean, we all know about Jimi Hendrix, Janis Joplin, Jim Morrison and all those people we loved. They all died from alcohol and drug abuse. They didn't die from the 1960s; they died from alcohol and drug abuse. The 1960s just happened to be something they were going through at the time.

I never really wanted much; I just wanted more. And I just kept going and going. I was the rat on the wheel. Scientists do experiments on them because they usually die after a certain point, and I did. I was killing my spirit, just killing it.

I remember a certain day in my life. It's a blur of powders and liquid, but I had been up for four days, driving all over the place high. It was the same thing that happened all the other nights, the same experience. I was getting as high as possible but there was never enough. There weren't enough cigarettes to smoke, there wasn't a joint long enough, there wasn't a line wide enough—there was just never enough. Anyway, I was living in a home I couldn't afford, this huge mansion up in the hills with an Olympic-size swimming pool. I had the whole thing. I was in the house waiting for the cocaine to come back and there were these strange people in my home. A guy was asking me if he could buy my car. It wasn't for sale. He might as well have asked me if I'd sell my wife; it was the same thing. And I considered it.

I wondered why all these people were in my home. I walked over to a mirror on the wall above the fireplace. I saw myself for the first time in a different light and I heard my head saying, *You're going to die if you don't stop this now. Where are you going to go with this? There's no place to go. You've been around the world a dozen times, you've been with beautiful women, you've been with successful people, you've had money. You have property, prestige, and here you are sitting in the living room three days later getting high with strangers.*

That night I went to a meeting and I've been sober ever since.

Stevie Ray Vaughan

*I was in heavy denial the last
seven years of my using. There was
a point when I thought I might have been
drinking too much, thought that I might
have a problem, but the people I hung
around with drank the same amount,
so it must have been my problem
that I couldn't handle it.*

A Few Words on
Stevie Ray Vaughan

I remember walking down the narrow concrete concave of the theater, turning the tight corner leading to the dressing room. Inside sat a man smoking a pipe. Next to him, in his trademark black fedora, the rim of which was covered with a fine layer of dust, sat Stevie Ray Vaughan. He greeted me with a smile and a handshake, and offered me a drink.

On a small table in the crowded dressing room sat a large bottle of whiskey and several glasses. Stevie picked up three glasses, swiftly poured a trio of drinks and handed one to me, one to his bassist, Tommy Shannon, and kept one for himself. It was February 1986, backstage at the Royal Oak Music Theater in Michigan directly following the

*afternoon sound check. Stevie Ray Vaughan and Double Trouble
headlined six sold-out nights at the theater.*

*I was not a whiskey drinker, never was. But when Stevie Ray
Vaughan offered you a drink, you took it. At least I did, back then.
Ninety minutes and several drinks later, I left with some great
quotes. Since I lived only minutes from the theater, I caught three
shows that week and spent more time backstage with the band.*

*During our next visit, ironically, we had something in com-
mon. We had both become sober. The beginning of my sobriety
was tough, but it was easy for me to open up to him. He was very
caring, and offered some potent advice. This was about six weeks
after I had talked with Steven Tyler. I didn't have a sponsor at the
time and Stevie Ray suggested I make it a point to find one immediately. Instead of slamming the thought down my throat by
preaching because he knew that I was putting it off, he spent a
long time explaining the benefits of having one.*

*We talked a couple more times following that conversation.
Once I knew this book was happening, I called his publicist and
scheduled an interview especially for these pages. I was looking
forward to sitting down with him at length, once again, to talk
about sobriety. I admired his recovery. Considering the intensity
with which he played his 1959 Stratocastor, Stevie Ray Vaughan
was a very gentle, caring person. He was extremely sincere. When
he talked with you, you knew that he was talking from his heart.
His quiet manner seemed to originate from his soul. It was a very
comfortable feeling. He was scheduled to play a concert in town
in October. We would sit down at length, his publicist promised.*

*Stevie Ray Vaughan died in a helicopter crash on August 27,
1990. He died a sober and happy man, filled with gratitude.*

*The following words are excerpts from a phone interview we
did just a few months before his death.*

I was constantly taking stuff for my stomach—everything: Pepto-
Bismol, Tagamet—and washing it down with Maalox. I was caus-
ing incredible damage to my stomach and was still unable to believe
I had a problem.

I got to the point where I could not imagine doing anything without drugs and alcohol because I didn't. If I was awake, I had it. If I

was awake, I was doing it and had been for a while. You pretty quickly whittle down what things you do not associate with it, and you stop doing those things.

I continued to stay awake for nearly two weeks when we were mixing the live album. I used all of the available resources that I knew would keep me in a constant state of awakeness—cocaine, alcohol, pills. Whenever I felt like sleeping, I'd do some more lines, and if I still felt like taking a break from working, I'd do some more.

We were mixing the album and touring at the same time. We thought we could do it all. I was sure I could handle the hectic schedule of both jobs. The secret for me was not to get any sleep at all. I would play a gig, then stay in the studio all night mixing the album and selecting the material. I'd leave the studio around 11 A.M. or noon, grab a shower and wash up at the hotel. Then I'd go do the sound check and play the show. I'd then start the process all over again.

If we were tired or run down, there'd always be a hit for us to take. I did so much coke and drank so much alcohol in those two weeks, I'm amazed it didn't kill me. That's all I lived on during that time. That was my diet. The chemicals wacked out my perspective. I couldn't think straight. I was acting with the insanity of an addict. I never even thought about taking one or two days off. That was my way of thinking during that period. Thank God I know a different way of thinking now.

My body would start to twitch—you know, the nerves in my neck and arms—and I'd swallow some more alcohol to keep them quiet. I was throwing up blood and weird stuff a lot, but I had always done that when I used a lot. I didn't think much of it. I knew that I could beat the odds and mix this album in record time. I thought I could conquer it all, but it was the same with everything else. I thought I was Superman, I really did because if somebody said, "Man, this is tough, it's hard to do," I'd go, "Well, give it to me, give me that thing, I'll show you how to do it."

I also turned into a very bad person. I never knew the meaning of the word gratitude until I became sober and discovered the program. In the last five years of my drinking and using, my career was becoming more and more successful, but I never really saw it. I never really appreciated it.

I had reached a place where I couldn't stand myself. Every once in a while I would do something I felt okay about and I would want to be okay, but I couldn't. It was getting to where every once in a while I was taking a break from doing shitty things and doing something I liked or doing something that was okay or something that was good, as opposed to screwing up every once in a while.

The drug problem, the alcohol problem and all the fear involved were symptoms of a much larger problem, an underlying problem—and that's lack of love. Once you cross that line and become an addict or alcoholic, the drugs and alcohol replace the people that you care about and people who care about you. Love abandons you. You forget the basics of love, how to love and how to accept love. Your entire being becomes consumed by fear.

I was in heavy denial the last seven years of my using. There was a point when I thought I might have been drinking too much, thought that I might have a problem, but the people I hung around with drank the same amount, so it must have been my problem that I couldn't handle it. I would never blame myself for any of the problems in my life; I would always point the finger. It was always the wrong girl or the wrong producer or the wrong sound engineers. If I was using on one particular occasion and I didn't feel right, I blamed it on the drug. I thought I was taking the wrong drug. Or it was a bad batch of coke. Or I was drinking the wrong alcohol. Or I should have eaten before I drank. You know, saying everything I could to blame my present state of feelings on something else. It was always the outside that was at fault. Truth is, I was living in my little guarded world of denial. I've since learned that everything is controlled from the inside. I didn't know that.

You know, when I was six years old, I was a good little kid. Somewhere along the way my thoughts changed. I became terrified. Much of my adult life was lived in total fright. The drugs and the alcohol had a wonderful soothing effect; they quieted my mind of the fear. Somewhere deep inside was the little six-year-old wanting to get out, but I could never be honest with myself, honest with my thoughts. That was this powerful monster called denial.

Meetings are what saved my life, what give me strength. They show me that I'm not the only person in this world that has to fight this disease. They give me the tools I need to maintain healthy sobriety. A lot of times meetings are on our itinerary. It'll already have the central group number and usually one of the crew gets there first. There are two people in the crew who are in the program, too, and they usually get there ahead of us. If there's a meeting that we can make, we probably know about it early on.

Sometimes we can be a lot more open because there are four of us; we can have our own meeting. We've seen most of each other's bullshit and we've watched each other walk through it. We're still walking through it, so we can help each other.

Meetings eliminated my denial. I can now look this right in the face and stare it down. It's like, *Okay, I'm diseased, I can't drink or do drugs anymore, so now what? What am I going to do to fill that hole where there's the lack of love and the emptiness? How am I going to handle these emotions that have been bottled up inside me for the last 10 years?* Meetings slowly and subtly remove my fears. The more I attend, the better I feel. That's why if we can't make a meeting in the town, we're fortunate enough to have our own meeting.

I've got this bag—I call it my bag of bricks—it's full of recovery books I carry with me. I go through phases. I mean, I try to take some of them out. I'll put a stack out and put this one over here and maybe leave this one home today, or I'll end up with maybe two or three books less; then I'll go to the bookstore. But you know, when I'm getting a jam inside, I start hitting my knees because I'm crazy. I go with it and I feel real good and then I start slacking off and I start looking everywhere I can for something that makes sense.

If you can maintain that strength and discipline in reading recovery books, and attend meetings on a regular basis, you're gonna take care of it. It's only when you start slacking off that this disease creeps up on you. You won't even know it's happening, then suddenly you'll react in a crazy way, and all the time you spent in recovery will be lost for that moment.

Continue to read books, go to meetings and develop an honest relationship with your sponsor. There are so many people who at first are scared to ask someone to sponsor them. They're missing out on one of the main elements of recovery. There are all kinds of reasons why you should have a sponsor. A lot of them you don't get at first, you don't find out why until a long time down the road. When you keep tripping over the same hurdles, and you finally realize you've been tripping over them, you know because you don't always fall on your nose when you trip over one.

If you are rigorously honest with your sponsor, go to meetings and read some strong recovery books, you'll see rewards you've always dreamed of. You'll be out of your denial, and the treasures will unfold right before your very eyes.

Chapter 111

THE BIG
CRASH

They took me to the hospital,
But I swore I wouldn't go.
My blood was very much too high,
My heart was much too slow.
The doctor had some questions,
Some things he had to know.
The lady shook her head and said,
"The boy's got no control."

—Eddie Money
"No Control"

For many of us, the reality of this disease never sets in until it's too late. A great number of alcoholics need to hit bottom before they accept responsibility for their downfall. For years, they've been blaming someone else or some other thing; rarely do they examine the source. It's easier to blame others than to face the music.

After years of using and abusing, we hit our bottom. We are emotionally and physically drained.

Reality has set in. Many people in this book believe that you're lucky if you've hit bottom and survived.

Jack Scalia was literally a heartbeat away from certain death as he stood on the 12th-floor window ledge of a German hotel, counting the seconds before he jumped to the pavement some 120 feet below.

Tai Babilonia hit bottom hard with a suicide attempt.

Ritch Shydner's body was literally repulsing the amount of toxins it held. He spent more than a week detoxing the poison.

Mitch Ryder battled an 18-year Valium addiction.

They all survived. They all made it through the horror and climbed to the top, to the fresh air and reality of their emotions. No longer clouded by their addictions, they are proof that no matter how deep your bottom may seem, you possess the ability to climb out of the crash and survive.

Jack Scalia

Jack Scalia is a recovering alcoholic and drug addict. He was the first-round draft pick of the Montreal Expos in 1973. After suffering a career-ending injury the following year, he became successful in the modeling world. It led to dozens of television movies and three television series: *Dallas, Devlin* and *Wolf.*

I had very low self-esteem, even though externally there were a lot of great things happening in my life. I didn't feel like I deserved it, so I was going to do everything in my power to destroy it.

I was up to about an ounce a week in coke and spending between three and four thousand a week. I generally drank a case of beer a day and all the insanity that goes along with that. My particular kind of addiction was one of extreme phases and paranoia, very violent. It was similar to *A Clockwork Orange* kind of thing. Either I was going to destroy something or in the process be destroyed.

I'd been arrested in San Francisco for drunken disorderly and assault. My career was falling apart in the modeling world. People said, "Yeah, Jack's a great guy, but we never know if he's going to show up and if he does, we don't know what kind of shape he's going to be in."

All the while I was self-deluding. I thought that nobody knew what I was doing. My fiancée broke up with me. I had alienated all my friends because of my violent behavior when I was using, and I was generally using all the time.

I anesthetized myself, even though I'd flip a car and be lucky that three people walked away from it. Or I'd get arrested or in a fight and I'd stab somebody, or somebody would cut me or put a gun barrel to my mouth. Somehow that didn't mean anything because a couple days later I was doing the same thing. That's part of the insanity and part of the self-deluding that goes on.

I used to start when I took a shower. I'd have the vial in the soap dish over the sink and I'd have a towel above my head on the curtain rod. I'd dry my hair and my face off and stick out my head and do a few hits to get me started in the morning. That was generally after passing out the night before from drinking so much beer.

The thing I dreaded the most was seeing the sunrise. That meant I'd pulled an all-nighter. It was like the vampire experience with the sun. It was also another way of telling me that I had screwed up. If I managed to get some sleep somehow, I could rationalize that I was okay, but I would see the sun and say, *Damn, I have a whole day ahead of me. Now what am I going to do?*

I'd do the coke to get me going in the morning and then I'd take a cab to my dealer's place and do a gram. That was generally around eight, and if I had a job I was on the way to, I'd stop by the grocery store and pick up two or three cans of beer. I'd drink them on the way to the job to take the shakes off. I'd still have another gram to get me through the job, then after the job was finished I'd go cop again.

When I was in baseball, I dropped acid in spring training. On top of that, I had injuries and the doctor prescribed a muscle relaxer. A muscle relaxer is fine if you take it in the prescribed amount, but I would take a 30-day supply in 8 or 9 days and drink on top of that, which would magnify everything that was happening to me.

It all goes hand in hand with the sense that I was on a self-destruct mission, not feeling that I deserved any of this. I was the number one draft pick. And I had very low self-esteem, even though externally there were a lot of great things happening in my life. I didn't feel like I deserved it, so I was going to do everything in my power to destroy it.

To kill the pain, they put me on pills or they'd shoot me up to get me to pitch. Had I been a little more level-headed about it, or prepared better in life for some of the pressure that goes along with that kind of thing, I could have said, "Look, my back is really in bad shape; you know that. I'm crawling around on my hands and knees. Why don't you just send me home for the last month, let my back heal, and I'll come back better next year." But I didn't have that belief in myself, or the self-esteem or courage to even speak up for myself.

At 20, 21, there is no mortality. We all feel immortal. My nickname was Superman. I don't know if I believed it, but at that age you're not thinking of much. I know I wasn't, and it snowballed. When I had the arm surgery and found that my arm popped, I knew I was finished. In a way, my nightmare came true. I finally destroyed something that was going well in my life.

I had a very crazy childhood. In some regards I had a very happy childhood, but in other ways it wasn't so. There are blocks of years I don't remember at all. I don't really remember in detail, say from 7 to 9 and from 11 to 15. I remember little things, but not much. There was no reason for me to remember. There was less pain in my life if I didn't deal with it, so that's the route I went. That's what my drug addiction and alcohol use was. The more drugs I put into my body, the less pain I felt. I was making over six figures a year for two or three years, but I had no money.

I took a job doing a modeling assignment in Germany so I could get enough money to get into rehab. I got to the job and I was fine. I said, *I'm going to keep myself straight,* but they were having their Oktoberfest and we started to drink. I got back to my hotel and I ordered 24 bottles of beer, but they wouldn't send up 24. They said they could only send up 12, so I had them send up 12 and I called right back down again and they sent me 12 more.

I just started drinking and the next thing I knew I was on the window ledge of the room I was in on the 12th floor. I called a friend in New York and told him where I was and what I was going to do. I said, "I've got to get into a rehab," and he said, "I'll look into it and call you back in a half hour." I said, "Call me back in 15 minutes. If you call back in 16 I won't be here to answer the phone."

I was standing on the window ledge and the window was open. I was on the outside. I heard a voice, and to me the voice was God. He said, "Before you do what you're going to do, let me show you your life." He gave me like a videotape of my life and said, "Okay, now I'm going to give you a choice. If you're going to continue doing what you've been doing in your life, then you might as well step off. But if you want to change, just step back and reach out. I'll be there for you."

I don't remember stepping back or down or anything. I just knew I had the phone in my hand and I was standing next to the desk and my friend said, "You're in the day after tomorrow. Come home." Two days later I was in rehab.

I felt like I was home. I had arrived. I found a place where I'd be safe. Somebody knew the hell I'd been in; it wasn't just me. My problems weren't unique and I wasn't alone. My whole reason for talking about it is not to wave the flag of Jack Scalia because my flag was one of self-destruction. I figure that in God's ultimate plan, he kept me around for a reason. People like me and Gregory Harrison and Lou Gossett Jr. and other people who have not only made a commitment to stay sober, but also to help as many people as we can, God kept us around.

I talk about it to let people know how to spread the message and say, "Hey, you're not alone, the problem you have is not unique. There is a way out of the living hell, but the only way you can be helped is: you have to reach out."

If you're being swept down a river, people could be sticking their hands out or throwing life preservers with a rope attached to them, sticking out a pole. If you keep your hands in your pockets, all of these things mean nothing. You have to reach out and grab one. That's the only way you can be pulled to the shore.

Tai Babilonia

Tai Babilonia is a recovering alcoholic and drug addict. She's a world-champion figure skater who, along with her partner, Randy Gardner, won numerous awards for her world-wide performances.

The key thing for me was: you have to clean house. I went through my phone book and eliminated all my drinking buddies. You can't be around them. I cleaned my phone book out. I stopped going to my old hangouts. If you're serious about it, you just can't go to the old bars, the old nightclubs. I did a complete turnaround.

It started with a glass of wine. I was out on the road with the touring show for nine months out of the year. It was a whole different life for me, as opposed to competing when you have your parents there and you have everyone doing things for you. As an amateur, all you do is skate, but when you turn professional and you're out on the road, city to city, they're not there. I was sort of lost and very lonely, very depressed, and couldn't sleep at night. That one glass of wine was my way of getting away from what I couldn't deal with. Then that glass of wine turned into heavier liquor.

I didn't know that there was a problem. I just knew that taking the alcohol was helping me deal with touring. I didn't realize how bad it was until toward the end in 1988, when I pretty much hit rock bottom and things were getting real ugly. I was also taking amphetamines, which is a deadly combination: uppers and alcohol. Up and down; the roller coaster. My moods were crazy.

On the ice the timing was not there. Being in a pair team, you have to match your partner. Some days we were okay and some days we were awful. A couple of nights I was out in front of an audience and I couldn't remember the routine. I couldn't remember what the next step was or what the next element was in the number. I literally had to ask Randy while I was out there in front of people what was next, and that was scary. That went on for a little while.

I really don't know how I got through it. Someone was obviously watching over me because it's so dangerous, especially with all the lifts and throws and different maneuvers, and me under the influence. That's pretty dangerous for both of us.

The last tour in 1988 was pretty much up and down. I was always saying, "I want to go home," and "I'm not going to finish the rest of the tour." Randy talked me out of it. I had to finish it because I had signed a contract. To break that contract would have been disastrous. But I got through it, and when I finished, I said, "I have to take a break. I have to take time off. I'm sick and I need help."

I announced that I was retiring because I was fed up with the same old lifestyle. I hated skating, didn't want to have anything to do with it. I got really depressed. That's when I tried to take my life. I hated the one thing I worked for all my life. A lot of that was the alcohol playing with my mind. There comes a time in your life when you say, *Hey, I'm a grown-up and I should deal with these things.* I got myself a good shrink; therapy has helped. I'm not as hard on myself as I used to be. It's okay to make mistakes. We all make mistakes and try to correct them. You don't have to correct them right away; it takes time and it's a process. Just like getting sober, it doesn't happen overnight. It's okay to be imperfect and it's okay to fail.

I think the key thing for me was: you have to clean house. I went through my phone book and eliminated all my drinking buddies. You can't be around them. I cleaned my phone book out. I stopped going to my old hangouts. If you're serious about it, you just can't go to the old bars, the old nightclubs. I did a complete turnaround. I was living in West Hollywood, which is crazy enough, and I moved to Santa Monica, which is a little slower paced, not as crazy.

You have to do whatever it takes. Everyone's different. I sort of just closed myself in my apartment for awhile. It was hard those first few weeks, the first month. I went crazy, but I was so determined, and so afraid to go back to my old self. I didn't want that. A lot of what helped me was my discipline with skating. That determination—it's like setting goals, and I started to use that.

I was still afraid of the past and what had happened and how I had hurt people and hurt myself, so that was always in the back of my mind. I was scared. It scared the shit out of me.

With my sobriety, skating is fun again. It feels the way it felt when I was a kid. I haven't felt that way in a long time. There's a freeness now, which toward the end was not there. Toward the end it felt like there was a ton of bricks on my back. Now that my head is clear and I'm not so hard on myself, Randy and I have the best time out there. We both feel it; we've got that connection again. We're able to communicate again mainly because I'm more on top of things now.

If you want to get your life together, you have to make some changes.

Ritch Shydner

Ritch Shydner is a recovering alcoholic and drug addict. A Los Angeles-based comedian, he's made several appearances on the *Late Show with David Letterman* and *The Tonight Show.* He continues to tour the country with his act and is working on several television projects.

I remember being up at ten in
the morning, me and this other guy.
He was looking at me, saying,
"How do we stop, Shydner?" And I said,
"We can't stop. We can't with the power
of cocaine. You don't fucking stop."
But in my head I kept screaming.
I was just begging to stop.

I had just done my second Carson and I was close to a complete wreck on it. I was very angry and I came out defensive. I came out like a gunfighter. You know: pulled my jacket back and stalked out. Not a very

39

friendly approach to the comedy thing. Then I backed into the curtain like I didn't trust the audience. I was one of those gunfighters backing out of a saloon. It was not a great set. I had cocaine in my pocket because I wanted to know I had the security there in my pocket.

I had stopped drinking and doing drugs two days before so I could try to get control and try to clean up. Then I got drunk immediately afterwards and went to Ann Arbor, Michigan, and worked a club there. I said, *I'm not going to do any cocaine,* and I got blackout drunk every night drinking with this guy named Fritz at the Heidelberg Inn. He was German and I think he must have been an old SS officer. We'd sit down at the bar all night and he'd tell me stories. I can vaguely remember Panzer divisions rolling across Europe. "Ve had zem! Ve had zem right vhere ve vanted zem!" I'm drinking schnapps with this guy and I didn't touch cocaine all week. I thought I was doing so great, but I was blackout drunk every night.

Then I did it, the last night I was in Ann Arbor. I just went off on cocaine again. That's what I would do back then: I would quit one drug and do more of another. If I quit cocaine and alcohol, I'd smoke pot 24 hours a day. It was like rotating bald tires on a car. It didn't matter where I put them. I was not doing well.

It just got worse. I kept trying to quit, but I couldn't quit. I was in the Improv here in L.A. every night, sitting at the bar saying, "I have to quit drinking—give me another shot," then doing blow. I guess I howled enough because one of the women who worked there was sober and she told this other guy, who came up and said, "I want to take you to your first meeting. Do you want to go? You want to quit drinking?" And I said, "Yeah." I nearly fell off the stool laughing. "Yeah, I want to quit drinking."

He took me to a meeting and I had 44 days sober, but it was kind of like my way. I went to meetings, but I didn't get a sponsor because I was too afraid to ask anybody. You know: the fear of rejection. I didn't read the book or do the steps. I just went to meetings and had 44 days. You start to feel that the kid's back because you've been physically beat. They say when you hit your bottom, you go spiritually first, then emotionally, then physically. I just couldn't drink and do drugs anymore. I was just beat.

I went to play a club in Atlanta and I was telling these guys, "I'm not drinking; 44 days and no drinking." They're like, "We heard, Ritch. The word's out. No problem." And they're all up there partying in the office after the show. They're all drinking and the coke dealer's there and I'm sitting there smoking my Camels and drinking my Coca-Cola's. I'm hanging with them and I'm not drinking with them and the waitress brings over another tray of drinks. They all take their drinks and there's a Heineken left on the tray; my Heineken. *Well, no sense wasting this extra beer,* I thought. I just didn't think twice. I grabbed it, took a couple of sips, got the cocaine and was off. I was weakened. I almost killed myself. I really couldn't stop.

I hadn't been to sleep much of that week in Atlanta. I remember being up at 10 in the morning, me and this other guy. He was looking at me, saying, "How do we stop, Shydner?" And I said, "We can't stop. We can't with the power of cocaine. You don't fucking stop." But in my head I kept screaming. I was just begging to stop. He finally went home. I made him take the coke with him because I just couldn't take anymore unless we had needles. I put some in a cigarette but that didn't do anything and we didn't have anything to freebase it with, so I told him to get the fuck out of there and just take it home. He went home to his wife and I lay in bed, trying to sleep.

The club owner had this kid come get me and drive me to another gig. I was shaking and sweating, had the air conditioner turned all the way up. I stood up and tried to walk around. I couldn't even dial the phone. I wanted to call people and I couldn't even pick up the phone. I was thrown into the back seat of a car to go to another gig and I couldn't move. I was bloated. I remember blood coming out of everywhere, where it shouldn't be coming out. I was just toxic sweating. I told him I couldn't move. He had to help me into the back seat of this car, and he was so thrilled to see me. He said, "Danny told me I get to drive you over here. You're my favorite comic." And I was throwing up, saying, "Please don't touch me, no, no, no," and he said, "I have to take you to this club." I kept saying no. I was crying. I just wanted to stay there.

It flashed in my mind about Hank Williams. I had read his biography and that's what I thought: I thought I was going to die. My heart was doing palpitations and I was sweating, on the verge of death, I thought. I was moaning and had him pull over. I threw up on the road and I threw up in his car. He drove me to the gig and I had to go on stage that night.

I did one of the worst shows I've ever done. Got on stage and did, I think, 20 or 30 minutes. I was headlining this gig and I couldn't stay up there long. I was sick. I was just toxic sick. I tried to drink coffee and threw that up. I was toxic that whole week. I'd go do a show and I'd go back to the hotel and I would just sweat and eat. I ate a lot of pizza and carbohydrates, just ate a lot of junk. I thought I was going to die that whole week. I was detoxing from the cocaine and the booze.

I came back to California and drove right from the airport to the Improv to see this woman who was a friend of mine. I told her what happened and she said she saw it in my face. She said that I was shattered, and I was. I said, "I have to do something different. I need a sponsor." And this guy who's really well known around here—Mickey Bush—well, Mickey was at the Improv that night. My friend Claudia said, "Why don't you go ask him?" and I said, "I can't." Then Mickey came by.

I was afraid to ask him, but he was the guy that I wanted because he was laughing. I couldn't laugh anymore. I was a comedian who couldn't laugh. Nothing was funny. I'd go to meetings and I was terrified. I couldn't laugh. I either hated people or I was terrified of them.

My shows weren't funny. Nothing was funny. This guy was laughing at meetings, this big, loud laugh, and I said, *I want to have fun like this guy. That's all I want.* He was a big attraction. I saw him at my first meeting. I remembered this guy and he told a big funny story and everybody was laughing. I got angry at him because he was funny and I wasn't, and I'm supposed to be funny.

This is how God works, it's amazing. He was at the Improv that night and he came up and said, "I hear you need a sponsor." I just blurted out, "Would you be my sponsor?" He goes, "You're on, mate."

I went to a lot of meetings. Sometimes two or three a day. I wasn't very employable, so I had the time. All I did was just go in there. By going, by showing my face, taking my body in there, the people knew I wanted help. They came and they put their arms out to me and gave me their numbers. I came home from meetings with all these numbers and threw them in the wastebasket. I thought I didn't deserve anyone's attention, like if I called them up I'd be bugging them. I didn't deserve their help, but they kept giving me their numbers and they kept supporting me. After a while it's neat because we all want that attention. We all want people to go, "Hey Ritch, how you doing?" I'd come into meetings and there'd be people going, "Hey Ritch." I don't care who you are, when people recognize you and see your face and they smile and wave to you, it's so great. That's what made me keep coming back.

People were laughing a lot there. Then I started getting the joke, and that was great. When I hear people talking about their episodes— you know, normal people hear of our episodes and they're shocked; but you get a room full of alcoholics and addicts, and we're just rolling with laughter.

I thought for sure I was done doing comedy. I thought positively the party was over and there was no way that I was going to be able to perform straight. I had to keep going back on stage and going to meetings and meeting other people who did what I did. Seeing them doing it is what gave me the faith. It was like, they did it. Although there were seven voices in my brain going, *You're done, you're not as good as them, you're not as funny, you're really stupid, you're from a small town,* these other people did it: they kept going back. I wasn't having a great time performing because I didn't have the old backup. Before, when I came offstage I could start drinking and doing drugs, all that stuff to take away the fear.

The other night I was on stage and I was doing material that I had done before a lot of times, but I was doing it differently. I was finding new places. I felt like a jazz player must feel or a guitarist when he starts running different notes in a song he's played a number of times and he's finding different ways of playing them. I was so high, it was unbelievable. I was acting out stuff and I was going further in acting out the stuff than I normally do in my act. The crowd just kept going with me, and the laughs were building up higher.

When I came off, the bartender, who is an actor, said, "I've never seen any performer act the way you just acted. I've never seen any comedian in here do what you just did, and I've been here since the place opened. You just took everything you've been doing and you went a whole new level with it. You were doing new stuff that was terrific."

But even on the worst nights and with the hardest crowd, it's nothing compared with what it used to be. I'm still here and there's no fear. I'm never going to do that again.

When I was drinking and using, I had fistfights with audience members. It was insane. I used to tear people up. I'd look for them. And now it's just the opposite. I had a woman say the harshest thing I ever had anybody say. It was in San Diego. I was having one of those dream nights. The place was just roaring. People were asking me questions and playing, and this woman goes, "One question." I go,

"Sure." She goes, "Where did you find a cunt dumb enough to marry you?" It was the most evil statement I ever heard. The place chilled. Unbelievable. But I didn't put her down. Then somebody quickly changed the subject.

Later, some other guy heckled over near where this woman heckled before. He heckled me a few times, so I went over to talk to him. I said, "I'm going to get a good look at you," but I really wanted to get a look at her. I didn't want to go offstage before when she said that because it would look like I was physically coming after her. I didn't want to do that. I just wanted to get a look at her.

So I went walking over. I saw him and I played with him. Then as I was walking back, I said, "By the way, where's the woman who doesn't like my wife?" Two people who were at her table pointed her out. She was sitting in front of all these empty bottles and shot glasses, drunk, with the saddest look on her face. I knew that she was a practicing alcoholic. You just saw it, the booze and the bloat, the whole thing. She had a cigarette in her mouth and I looked in her eyes and they were dead. I didn't say anything. I just turned around and walked back to the stage. I felt it. I thought, *Wow, that's where I was heading.* She couldn't understand what was going on. She was just gone.

You know, the funny thing is that for a long time I thought I feared failure. I found out something. I feared success. I don't fear it anymore. I read somewhere that the reason we fear success is we can't control it. We can control failure. I can guarantee that when I'm drinking and doing drugs, I know how to be a failure. I've got the formula down and I can repeat it. But success—how are we going to hold onto it and control it? I don't have to control it anymore.

I didn't feel I deserved it because I knew the kind of person I was. I was a cheat, a liar, and like any alcoholic, whenever I wanted what I wanted my plan was to get what I wanted and who cares about how I got it? I never felt good about that because I always went the short route in any way I could. I never was willing to stick in for the long haul and just take my time and enjoy what I was doing. I just wanted the end. I didn't care about the trip, the journey to it. Just get me to the end. When you have that attitude, you cheat and you lie, and you're not good to yourself and people around you. You don't feel like you deserve all that stuff.

There are going to be different levels of success. I've been successful in the last several years; it just keeps blossoming. It just keeps getting better, and now I have a relationship with my wife that I never had before. I never had any kind of relationship like this. It's not perfect, but I've never had honest communication or monogamy before now.

I don't act out on the old stuff because I have too much at risk in this relationship. It means so much. And the product of that is in the other room sleeping: that's my daughter. That's the greatest. This is a big success here; we're buying this house. I paid for this stuff, my wife and I, largely through jokes! We get paid for jokes. If that's not a blessing! So whatever happens in my career level, I don't know what the turns are going to be, but I'm more able to adapt now than I ever was before.

Here's a chance for us to start a generation of kids growing up alcoholic who may be exposed to it, but they're growing up to know some things about it and about themselves and their parents. They will know about this disease. Genetically, my daughter is predisposed to having alcoholism, and she's gonna know what to do with that. If she has the disease, recovery is something she grew up with. It is a miracle to know that it all ends here. That she'll never have to see us drunk and will never have to put up with all the craziness that goes along in an alcoholic household. She's being raised in a house of recovery.

Mitch Ryder

Mitch Ryder is a recovering alcoholic and drug addict. He released a
string of hits throughout his career—
"Good Golly Miss Molly," "Devil
with the Blue Dress" and "CC
Rider"—and continues to perform
and release new material in the
United States and throughout Europe.

*I was in love with the star that
I had become. A lot of people cared very
deeply for me. They made great sacrifices
for me out of love. But they weren't
rewarded. I ignored them because
the persona of Mitch Ryder had
become the most important
thing in my life.*

Once I became addicted to Valium, of course I
needed it. I physically craved it. I can't really even
tell you why I began to take it except that there was a
period in my life when I had just cut the *Detroit* album

and we had worked very hard at getting that album together. It took two years to get to the point where we made the album. The band toured behind it for another year and the album didn't happen. It had every right to happen. It was a very powerful album.

The way we lived—our lifestyle—we were constantly smoking joints. I remember waking up in the morning and it would be the first thing I'd go for, a joint. I couldn't imagine it being any other way. It wasn't just that, but the drinking, the acid, all the stuff we did as a group, too. We had this image we actually lived. It wasn't a press creation. When they wrote things about us being dangerous and partiers, it was all true. We were that way.

That lifestyle was even more fervent and more consuming than the years I spent on the very top of my career as a star in America. I just burned out on it. I quit the band and, having quit, I didn't really want to get into another band. I was frustrated because I couldn't earn money any other way. I didn't have royalties coming from publishing because they had been taken from me.

I got involved in another band, which was a bunch of drug-crazy people, too. It seemed like every time I would try to meet with musicians or get together in a band, there was always this thing where everybody was high all the time. I couldn't get away from it. So rather than fight it, I did what everybody else did. I continued to use drugs.

I quit that band for the same reasons: the frustration of not going anywhere and not being straight enough to enjoy what I was doing. I thought the only way I could enjoy things was to get high again. So Valium was an offshoot, my nervous system reacting to all the different chemicals I was injecting, but I didn't tell the doctor that. I just told him I was real nervous, and he did whatever doctors do to check you out. He did everything except take a blood check for the drugs that were in my system. He wrote me the prescription and that started a cycle that went on until a few years ago. It began in 1973. That's how long I was on Valium. I was very, very addicted to it.

In the hospital they had to wean me with other Valium-like equivalents. I forgot exactly what they used, but you can't just withdraw from Valium because your body will go into shock and seizures. It had to be pretty heavy; they had to clean my blood out gradually instead of just pulling it off. The pity of the whole thing is that so many Americans have prescriptions for Valium.

There were deals being made and I was apparently signing things

I don't remember. I looked at a piece of paper recently; it appeared back in my life. It was one of those agreements that I had written when I was in a drunken state. I granted this particular person the world-wide rights for a video he had shot. As I recall, I needed 30 dollars to get something and at that particular time I didn't have it on me. It wasn't about me being broke, it was just that I needed it at the moment. I said, "Well, if you give me this until later, you can have what you want." And he, being the clever dude he is, suggested it. I realized that it was ridiculous to give him that right even when I did it, but because I was deeply into my alcoholism I thought, *Why not. That'll be cool.*

But that's just one of the many agreements that I entered into. Some were agreements that contradicted other agreements during the course of my binges and my alcoholism, my drug addiction. What happened was my respect for myself, my career, my value, my esteem, my ego, were all on a downward slide. The less respect I had for myself, the less respect I had for any business decisions I had to make. I would call a meeting, but I wouldn't go unless they met me in my favorite bar so I could be comfortable. Everything took a back seat to being high. My career was damaged because of it. I'm still waging the battle to overcome the image, and probably will be the rest of my life. There were so many idiotic, irresponsible actions I suffered through at my own hands during the course of all that. Just horrible, horrible stories. They're not even worth repeating, except to illustrate that the burlesque was in full flower.

During a concert down in Texas, I stole some guy's hat. He kept begging me for an autograph and he wouldn't leave me alone. He came up tune after tune and I said, "All right, you want an autograph, I'll give you an autograph." I took his hat, a ten-gallon hat, and the band kept playing. I pulled my zipper down and urinated. Filled his hat and gave it back to him. He was seething. The stage was high above the ground; all you could see was him bouncing up trying to get high enough where he could get onstage and kill me. There are tons of stories like that and they're shameful. They're very, very shameful.

I can't name names, but the band that I've been with—some of these guys I've been with for 13 years—is infested with heroin addiction, alcoholism, everything that is bad for it. I'm now taking steps to remove myself from that situation finally because even though they'll respect my needs in terms of my sobriety—there's no beer now in the dressing room—they still insist on having their joints and drinks. They sneak around. They have a Coke can and go to the trouble of emptying the can and putting a mixed drink in it so they can have it onstage. They'll have paper cups that are reserved for water and they'll be filled with booze. They'll go out to the bathroom right before the show, but in fact what they're doing is smoking a joint or hash or shooting up. All this goes on.

The only thing that changed from my being sober is that they won't do it in front of me anymore. They think that their obligation to me is finished with that, but that's not true. Their obligation to me is the same obligation I have to them in regard to our profession. That is to be able to give 100 percent at any given moment we're called upon to do that. They still don't understand that if you're altering your consciousness or your nervous system with anything, you are not operating at 100 percent. They don't know that. They don't realize that. It's not a truism to them.

Recovery is so much more than just not drinking. A lot of people don't have the consciousness to achieve this awareness. Once you start the process, it's a process that should go throughout your life for the rest of your life. Eventually you'll end up being healthy in all ways. You won't want to stop with just addictions. You won't want to just take care of your mind. You'll want to take care of your soul. Once you start working on all these things and repairing them, you'll see results.

In the beginning you say, *I would like to be normal,* but then as you become healthier and healthier, you realize that the average person isn't that healthy anyway. Some people don't have these overriding addictions. They aren't abusive personalities to begin with. They still have their share of madness to deal with. People that are in recovery have a step over the people who have had healthy lifestyles all along because they're working at having a healthy life just like the other people are, but they're doing it with the knowledge of what it can be like. So it's like a plus to be a former abuser or a former alcoholic.

I've learned about the people around me and for the first time I'm able to conceptualize love. I was unable to do that before. I actually have a concept of what it's supposed to mean, what it's supposed to feel like and why I'm supposed to feel it.

I was in love with the star that I had become. A lot of people cared very deeply for me. They made great sacrifices for me out of love. But they weren't rewarded. I ignored them because the persona of Mitch Ryder had become the most important thing in my life. Keeping his existence and his image in the forefront became my daily effort. I became consumed by that and lost my self-identity on the way to that. I won't make that mistake again. It's hard, though, because every day I'm faced with it.

Chapter IV

COCAINE

We should be sleeping.
I'm wide awake,
but I'm dead on my feet.
We're never keeping
all of the promises
we said we'd keep.

—Eddie Money
"We Should Be Sleeping"

Someone once described cocaine like this: the second you do it, you want more. Dr. Steven Chatoff is the medical director of Exodus Recovery Center in Marina Del Ray, California. He has a remarkable way of explaining exactly how the drug controls various parts of your brain, making your system crave more; how its claws grab onto your body and mind, refusing to let go. His words are the informative scientific lesson people need to understand. Gregory Harrison and Larry Gatlin share their nightmares with the drug. They are among the few who have experienced a habit of such immense magnitude and lived to tell about.

Dr. Steven Chatoff

Dr. Steven Chatoff is a recovering alcoholic and drug addict. He is the medical director of the Exodus Recovery Center in Marina Del Ray, California.

Every cocaine addict you talk to says that one day he crossed over the imaginary line. One day it was not an option. It went from being one of the coping mechanisms, one of the tools to deal with in life, to being a necessary, dominant tool. They had to have it. On that day, a genetically predisposed biochemical imbalance was triggered.

In my experience, having treated a couple thousand patients now—addicts of all different drugs of choice and types of mixtures—nothing is as quickly addictive and quickly accelerated in terms of digression as cocaine. People tend to crash and burn. They go through the stages of social abuse and enter into the realm of addiction quicker than with any other drug. Quicker than heroin, quicker than alcohol, quicker than any pills, any combination thereof, quicker than PCP. What is really significant is that cocaine has something other drugs don't have. It tends to get its hook in quicker and cause debilitative effects; both mental and physical breakdown. The thought process becomes impaired more quickly. Paranoia is accelerated more quickly.

These things do happen with other substances, but sometimes it takes decades. The average length of time for a cocaine addict to really hit a significant dysfunctional bottom is less than two years, whereas a heroin addict may take seven to ten years.

Cocaine has been around for a very long time. In the beginning of the century it was in vogue and became known as the killer that it is. It's gone in and out of style through the decades. It returned in the 1980s as a nonaddictive sophisticated substance for the wealthy. Unfortunately, that allowed it to creep back into society as a quasi-acceptable substance that was a safe, social lubricant. Which is a bunch of shit. In reality it turned out to be the most addictive substance known to mankind.

As a social lubricant, it can be used in business. A lot of people, especially in Los Angeles and New York, feel at first that it helps them in the business world, that it makes them work longer hours, that it makes them more attentive to what's going on. Their income may actually increase, which is an unfortunate reinforcement for the drug. As their disease progresses from the social stage to the abusive stage—when the drug starts abusing the person—then people start using it not as they do in the social stage, where drugs and alcohol are kind of an option, but as a coping mechanism to deal with life. What happens in the abusive stage is that cocaine becomes the dominant coping method; it becomes the first thought when one needs energy. It's the first thought when one needs to be on, when one has to look good, whether in the social or in the professional sphere. Every cocaine addict you talk to says that one day he crossed over the imaginary line. One day it was not an option. It went from being one of the coping mechanisms, one of the tools to deal with in life, to being a necessary, dominant tool. They had to have it. On that day, a genetically predisposed biochemical imbalance was triggered.

One recent study showed that up to 92 percent of cocaine addicts have a positive family history for alcoholism, drug addiction or related disorders. That really points to the role of genetics—not just in cocaine addiction, but in all drug addictions. A person could be predisposed to this kind of time bomb in his body. One day he crosses over and that line is broken down through abnormal pathways. As that line is broken down, chemicals are secreted in the addict's body. Those chemicals are irritants that cause the cocaine addict to crave the drug. The craving is due to a biochemical imbalance; it is not a matter of willpower. It is not due to being a good or bad person. It's a chemical. Your willpower at this point is worthless.

It makes sense when you learn about the physiology of cocaine addiction. You see that cocaine, once you're in the realm of addiction, has an effect on the neurotransmitters of the body and involves your entire nervous system. Cocaine blocks the re-uptake of three important elements—serotonin, adrenaline and norepinephrine, the three substances that are necessary for a balanced state. Cocaine blocks the uptake, the reabsorption of these chemicals, across the neurotransmitters so that we are thrown into a severe biochemical imbalance. We are uptight and craving. Now the disease tells us that another line, which produces a very temporary short-lived euphoria, will make this better, when another line actually causes it to be even worse. That's the problem with cocaine addiction in particular. It's not so much that people long for the euphoria, it's that they long to be away from the dysphoria. That's very important.

Addicts feel they need some cocaine to deal with whatever they are about to do in life. They're craving the cocaine, then they get some and do it and go up very quickly. If they're basing it, they go up real quick, and they get that euphoric feeling, especially in the beginning, and then they come down. But when they come down, they come down twice as low as when they started. They started off doing not too great, but they went up and they came down much lower because the neurotransmitters have been blocked; they're worse off than when they started. This is why they must take another hit. This is why you see cocaine addicts do insane things to keep the run going.

The most basic human instinct is for the mother to feed her child. It's as primal and visceral as you can possibly get. I have seen many crack addict mothers go off on binges and leave their infants at home, forgetting all about them. That just puts me in awe of the power of cocaine. I've never talked to a heroin addict or alcoholic who has gone that far. I know many have nodded out and put their children in danger, but I've never seen heroin addicts who haven't fed their children. I've never talked with an alcoholic who has done that. They may not have performed the best parenting techniques, but never, totally, have they been self-obsessed with that insatiable need to get out of this bottom.

You see, cocaine users need to get out of the dysphoric feeling that comes from the rebound of the biochemically-induced euphoria. That's how people go off on these binges and end up living pitiful and incomprehensible predemoralized states, subhuman sometimes.

Cocaine addiction is really unique in its rapid onset and how quickly it gets its claws in you, how quickly you enter into the realm of addiction. The stages are really abbreviated; some people have no social and abuse stages. I know people who have become addicted immediately. I've never seen that with another substance.

I have treated patients who have never used anything in their entire lives. I'm talking Joe Normal, who went from high school to Harvard Undergraduate to Harvard Graduate School. CPA, Century City high-rise. Had a full firm, two German cars, house in the hills, wife, two kids, never drank before in his entire life. He started using cocaine at age 35 and crashed and burned in one year to no firm, no practice, no cars, no wife and kids, out on the street. One year. That's unbelievable. No other substance that I know can do that. And it's all because of the intensity of the craving and the obsession in the mind, which is biochemically induced.

Cocaine stresses the cardiovascular system intensely, every hit you take. Every hit raises the pulse rate and blood pressure, stresses the whole system. Anybody who has a genetic weakness somewhere or a defect of some kind, that area's going to be stressed. That's where we hear about strokes, which are fairly common in cocaine addiction. People don't eat well, they don't sleep. It's not just the drug itself, but the related behaviors that also tear down the heart and cardiovascular system—causing heart attacks, seizures and neurological damage to the point of one seizure after another until death. There is even a seizure that has been identified as a cocaine seizure; it is even treated differently and it's more deadly. ERs are flooded with them in major cities.

Your entire family and everybody who knows you is drawn into the instability of this disease and the downward spiral, the tornado of the cocaine addict. All of your morals, all of your commitments in life, both professionally and to your family, are thrown out the window. The biochemical need is so intense that it far outweighs any other priority in your life. It is totally dominating. I don't know anything else that is as quickly and totally dominating as cocaine.

I don't believe cocaine use has decreased one bit. I'm on the front lines. I not only treat patients in a lot of different settings, I teach counseling courses at high schools. I teach medical students at USC and UCLA and therapists in various graduate schools. All I get back is how much all their different modalities are being flooded with cocaine addicts. I don't hear of any decrease, at least not in this city.

We still have a tremendous drug problem in this country. The problem is people are dealing with their internal conflicts, their anxieties, depressions, unresolved grief and losses through the futile attempt of stuffing them through external fixes. Seeking external relief for internal conflict: that's the core problem. We're a society of quick fixes. I have an internal conflict, I'm going to fix it with an external means— drugs, alcohol, cigarettes, sex, compulsive overeating. Fix it now. That is a very false way of dealing with life.

Dealing with internal conflict effectively comes from processing it out, and processing our feelings is never a quick fix. That's part of the recovery process. People learn how to do that.

I see them crawl in barely alive. Then I see them go through the detoxification phase and watch them go through the changes that occur as the body rights itself biochemically—the mood swings, the impulse control problems, the need to be monitored during that period while their disease is calling them back out to the street. Then watching that pass. Then into rehabilitation, where they develop new coping mechanisms to be able to deal with life. Shit still happens on the street and their brain is going to say, *Try chemical relief one more time.* They have to know what to do instead: to connect with 12-Step support groups or aftercare programs, to see the light come back in their eyes and watch families come back together, to have the boss take them back, to promotions, to the three-month chip, the six-month chip, to see themselves take a cake and have to care as human beings again. It's beautiful for me to watch.

Of course, I also bury people. That goes with the turf.

I know that recovery works. I know that people do not need to die from cocaine addiction. The prognosis is very good for people who really do surrender to the fact that they have a disease, and are willing to go to any lengths and follow directions for staying clean and sober.

I'd say the success rate is somewhere around 80 percent. I think it's very high. I don't believe those doomsday statistics. People I know who will accept that they have a disease, that it's not willpower—they accept that they have a biochemical imbalance, that the gig is up, that they've used up the right chemical peace of mind, their body has changed. *Okay, teach me new coping mechanisms because I can't do that anymore.* They recover.

It's only the ones that are still trying to hold onto the reins and stay in the realm of willpower that die or continue to relapse until they have no choice.

Gregory Harrison

Gregory Harrison is a recovering alcoholic and drug addict. He's appeared in television's *Trapper John, M.D., Family Man, Falcon Crest, True Detectives* and *New York News* as well as several other television and theater projects.

People used to say,
"You have to stop and smell the
roses, Greg." I didn't even know what
they were getting at. Now I know. Now I
understand. I do stop and smell the roses.
I smell my kid's diaper and I love it.
I smell the good and the bad, and it all
smells sweet and alive. My feelings are
no longer anesthetized by a drug or
suffocated by impossible expectations.

It hooked me the first time I did it. I remember the very moment that I came onto this first tiny snort of cocaine at a party in the Hollywood Hills in 1978.

Within five minutes of snorting that one little spoonful of somebody else's stash—you know, *You gotta try it, it's really fun, it's great, it's harmless*—five minutes later I felt, for the first time in my life . . . perfect.

I had never felt perfect. I had always felt inadequate and like a failure. I thought I should be perfect. I was raised to strive for perfection and anything short of it was as good as failing miserably. I could get all A's, but if A+'s were available and I didn't get them, I was a failure. I was allowed to grow up judging myself by that standard. I carried it right into adulthood, into everything I did. I've never been perfect. I have never been able to achieve it. I've always felt like a failure no matter how good I was at anything. I've never felt like I was succeeding; there was an unspoken deep, deep, deep pain in me right up to that moment when I finally took my first snort of cocaine, and *that* was akin to finding God. I felt linked with perfection for the first time in my life. I was more handsome, more intelligent, quicker, more glib, wittier, stronger, more sure of myself. Everything that I ever wanted to be, I suddenly was, and I didn't even know how I'd arrived there. All I knew was when it went away again in half an hour, I knew I had been on the best ride of my life. I wasn't really sure what to attribute it to. I wasn't even sure if it was just a good mood that had hit me or what. I mean, I almost couldn't remember doing it, that little spoonful done on the run when somebody held it under my nose and walked away. I didn't really connect A with B with C, but I know that for all the rest of my addiction, I hunted for that perfection. Occasionally I found it to some degree when I used that drug, but for the most part I was a dog chasing its tail from that point on, always searching for that feeling I once had but would never have again.

That's the thing about cocaine: the first time that you come on to it, it's wonderful, and it's the last time that it's ever going to be that wonderful. But the interaction with your brain has happened and you're now going to chase it. Monkeys, given a choice between food and cocaine, will do the cocaine until they die of starvation. What does that tell you? I'm a monkey and that's what I tried to do. I was willing to kill myself for that drug and it was like that from the very first time.

I was never a user prior to that. I smoked dope and smoked hash and stuff in the Army during Vietnam, but that was just because I wanted out. I didn't want to be where I was, I just wanted to get away. Once I got out of the Army, I hated marijuana. It made me feel stupid, slow and unproductive, and I loved life. I loved the sharpness of feelings that I had and the challenge of the industry that I chose to try to make a living in, the odds being against me.

A month before I went into treatment, I was staying in my house here in Sherman Oaks, living in the gym section, this office/gym, a separate room on the opposite end of the house from the master bedroom. I was basically living in a silent arrangement with my wife. I'd stay in this room 24 hours a day. I guess I had been in there for about six months at that point, whenever I was in town. I was binging on cocaine and I would stay up anywhere from two to five days without sleeping, then finally succumb to my exhaustion and fall asleep on this couch I had in there.

I would sleep for 24 to 36 hours straight without waking up, and then I'd wake up in my own urine. I'd be so totally exhausted that I couldn't wake up, even to go to the bathroom, until I got enough rest to come to. My wife never came in. She has told me since I've sobered up that she was just waiting for the day when either I was going to have a heart attack and die or she'd walk in and I'd be hanging from the rafters. She figured I was on the verge of suicide; she could see what terrible misery I was in. Of course I never spoke about it because I never admitted to her I had a drug problem. I mean, in the midst of the most obvious drug problem probably ever known to mankind, I still was denying to my own wife that I had a drug problem. And I had had it for nine years at that point.

During that month prior to going to the Betty Ford Center, I knew I was full of shit. I knew I was abusing my money, my toys—no, actually my toys were abusing me now—that I was not able to pick up my 1½-year-old daughter because she didn't know who was picking her up. She never knew from one moment to the next whether I was trustworthy or not, whether I'd be friendly or have the shakes or be furious at nothing in particular or be paranoid or be whatever my mood swing was at the moment; so she unconsciously decided that maybe it would be a good idea not to be friendly with this guy. My own daughter didn't even want me to pick her up.

My wife and I were not communicating on any level, not even anger anymore—zip. I didn't exist in the house. I lived as if the rest of my family didn't exist in the house. We hadn't made love in two years. I'd been impotent for that entire time. I was taking 150 to 200 vitamins a day because I was so anemic. I was 35 pounds thinner than I am now and so anemic that I was trying to compensate for that with all these vitamins and special potions I'd get from health food stores. I was doing everything I could to keep my addiction alive—to keep me alive so that my addiction could stay alive. Such typical behavior; you do everything you can except quit the drug.

I had known for a couple years that I was a full-blown addict, but I never admitted it to anybody. I didn't understand addiction. I kept thinking it would be like when I once gave up smoking for three years. It took me four months to find the right time, and finally I did and then it worked. I was off it for three years, until I got a part where I had to smoke and then I got readdicted. I thought it was like that. *I'll just hang in there until the right time. I'll know when that time comes.* Well, I was losing my wife, my child, my money, my self-respect. My jobs were coming few and far between, my health was gone and I was about to lose my life. I can't imagine I would have survived more than another month because I was so sick and anemic, and still I was clinging to this theory that when the right time came I would clean up. I guess what happened was it became clear to me that I was going to die with my so-called pride intact; I never had to ask anybody for help. They could put it on my tombstone. And it was the most frightening, horrifyingly scary act I've ever done, I mean the most terrified I've ever been: picking up the phone and calling this clinic.

My wife had given me this phone number. I finally walked into her bedroom one night about three weeks before I went into Betty Ford, sat on the end of her bed at about three-thirty in the morning with a full gram up my nose—you know, the last gram I would ever do, I was sure. (I had promised myself again for the ten thousandth time, and it was only about 15 minutes before I left the house to go get another one.) I sat down at the end of her bed, woke her up, and in the dark I remember saying, "I need help. I need to go to a professional. I need to get some help. I'm going to die. I realize I'm going to die. I'm terrified. Do you know somebody who's been in a rehab center? Can you give me a phone number?" And she said, "I'll get you one." She did not say this in a friendly way, believe me. It was like, *No shit, Sherlock. I'll believe it when I see it.* In fact, she held that attitude for about six or eight months after my sobriety date. I had left a lot of wreckage.

The next day she found this number and gave it to me. I called them and they interviewed me over the phone. They said they were full, and would put me on a waiting list and let me know when something opened up. I think they said that it would be at least a month. I said, "You're kidding me. I'll be dead in a month." They said, "Well, we're sorry, sir, there's sort of a rush on this kind of a privilege you know, to get into rehab." Part of me was horrified. Part of me was relieved.

I went out immediately and started binging worse than ever. For three weeks I kept saying, *This is going to be my last, this is the last that I'll ever do so I can do all that I want, all that I ever dreamed of.* The oddest thing was going on in my head. I didn't understand it. I mean, I knew that I didn't want to be using anymore. I knew that if my true self had anything to say about it, I would stop as soon as I went in there and hopefully never do it again. And yet I bought more of it and did more of it and reveled in the self-destruction of it more that last three weeks than ever before. The oddest self-destruction thing to happen. It's amazing, like drowning in it.

I had bloody sores all over my body. I saw worms in my skin all the time, so I'd take these nail clippers and try to dig them out. I really was seeing these things. I had sores all over my face and my neck, and I particularly went for my genitals because of the impotence and the self-loathing, all associated with my lost sexuality. Now I understand some of it, but I almost semi-castrated myself. There was bloody Kleenex all over the floor of my gym every morning, where I'd been digging away at my testicles and digging away at my neck and my face. I mean, my sexuality is in my groin and my living is made from my face. I did everything I could to destroy both these things in my self-loathing.

Thank God that's over. Thank God my life has changed. I don't think about not using coke now. I don't think about not drinking. I don't think about how to stay clean. That happens because I've been thinking about how to be the best I can be, how to get the most out of life, how to taste it, smell it, see it, feel it, hear it, devour it as much as possible. I guess there's a second nature equation in my head that drugs equal disaster.

I remember a priest in Betty Ford who had been on the program, had a relapse, gone through Betty Ford and become sober. He came back for 30 days while I was in. He was sitting in the back of the room during one of the seminars. At the end he held up his hand and said, "I have just 14 days." He said, "I left Betty Ford nine months ago and

I had three months of sobriety and now I have 14 days. I've been out the whole time." He was this fascinating little guy with a clerical collar on, and he said, "All I want to say is listen to what they're telling you because it's true. Betty Ford does not," he said, "promise that you will be sober for the rest of your life. What they promise is they'll fuck it up for you for the rest of your life." And he said, "'Believe me, I went out there and I drank for five months and they fucked it up for me for the rest of my life."

We all laughed because here is this little holy man using that language, but the meaning struck home. What it is, is that old thing about ignorance is bliss. I understand the disease, and that's what the program does, that's what having friends around does when you're having your cravings: it reminds you of the intellectual knowledge that you have to keep reaching for. Just keep an intellectual understanding of it and you'll be able to survive it. I can't ever be ignorant again. If I ever want to get loaded again, I won't be able to do it with the same blind full-steam-ahead, *hey, I'm just out for some fun* attitude that I used to have. I'll be tormented from the moment I pick it up until I go back and sit at a meeting and get sober again.

I've come to realize that nobody else is going to make me feel perfect. Now I have a new concept for perfect. Perfect is the way my higher power has created this land and this world and this existence of ours, with all its ups and downs and ins and outs and apparent failures and successes. When you put it all together, it's perfect. When you put me together with all my foibles, that makes me perfect. I love my wife as much for the things that piss me off as I do for the things that make me laugh, and now I'm loving myself as much for the things that piss me off as I do for the things that make me happy. That I do, that I am.

I'm judging myself by a whole new standard. It is such a relief. Finding sobriety, going to meetings and following the program have allowed me to appreciate my imperfection. I hate to call it that because now I think I'm perfect—I'm perfectly human. For the first time in my life I feel this wonderful relief from the pressure of having to keep pushing and performing, searching for that impossible goal. And I can stop and relax.

People used to say, "You have to stop and smell the roses, Greg." I didn't even know what they were getting at. Now I know. Now I understand. I do stop and smell the roses. I smell my kid's diaper and

I love it. I smell the good and the bad, and it all smells sweet and alive and real. I have real feelings. They're no longer anesthetized by a drug or suffocated by impossible expectations.

You know, I'm a very lucky guy. I have gone to lots of meetings and I've witnessed a lot of guys for whom I swear sobriety is 100 times harder than it is for me. I think the fortuitous turn of events in my life was that I didn't become an addict until I was 28. I didn't become an addict from being an alcoholic or from using drugs abusively all my life. I drank when I was 11 and partied and all that, but I also spent a lot of time sober. Most of my life, up until the age of 28, I had real feelings. I became an adult and functioned in society. I strove for a very difficult and ambitious kind of career.

So when I became an addict, I knew what I had lost. I knew to what I wanted to return. Most people that I go to meetings with start drinking or using at the age of 13, 14, 15—whenever it happened—and they never stopped until they got sober one day. That's why they call them babies when they walk into sobriety because they literally have to go back to the age of 13 and grow up from there, and learn to live and how to function as adults in society. I had already done that, and I had lost it.

So when I did get sober, I knew right where I wanted to go back to and was able to do it. Not immediately, of course; there were steps taken in trepidation on my part. It was terrifying in many ways, but I honestly don't think it was as terrifying as it is for most of the people that I went through rehab with, and most of the people that I go to meetings with. I thank God for that every time it occurs to me.

Larry Gatlin

Larry Gatlin is a recovering alcoholic and drug addict. His band has been prominent in country music for the last 20 years.

I did pretty good for 17 days without cocaine. Then I went to Fort Worth and my disease began to talk to me. I saw this guy I had known for a while—he's a drug dealer—and my disease said, You've been a good guy. You've really been good. I'm so proud of you. Just do one gram. Just have some fun tonight. You're in Fort Worth, at Billy Bob's. Let it go. *So I did, and it turned into a three-day binge.*

When I arrived in Nashville, I was immediately thrown in with the most wonderful bunch of singers, songwriters, musicians, entertainers and drug addicts in the world. A lot of them are dear friends, and many of them are recovering now and have changed their attitudes about life. I got there and they were all stars. They were my heroes. I learned to write songs sitting at their feet, listening to these wonderful tunes in hotel rooms down-town, in private homes or beer joints, in little places where we'd gather out on the road. For the first five or six years of my life in Nashville—early 1970s—that was the rare era I was thrown into. They were stars, they were happening. That's who I wanted to be. That's what I wanted to be. I emulated everything they did.

Nobody ever had to hold me down, and I mean, holy cow, if some-body said, "Let's go have some fun," well, I was the first one to jump in the truck. It wasn't their fault: at that point in time we didn't know. In 1970 we thought cocaine was a recreational drug, that it was not habit-forming, that it was emotionally addictive but not physically addictive. Now we know it's the most addictive drug on the planet.

I was 24 years old. I could do dope all night long, get four hours sleep, get up the next morning, and go to Portland and do a show. I didn't really feel too horrible. Those things change as you get a little older.

I knew that my life wasn't right, but it didn't dawn on me that there was any other way at that point. I thought I was in it and that was it. The road to the bottom is sometimes a very slow, painful thing. Sometimes people reach their bottom wrapped around a telephone pole in a car. Thank God I didn't do that, but it was not much fun.

The binges that I went on were absolutely horrifying. I've had people leave me after three days and say, "Gatlin, we have to go get some sleep." I'd say, "Oh hell, come on, let's go have some fun; we're just getting started."

Once, in Lake Tahoe, I checked into Harrah's Hotel, went to the Star Suite, ate a bowl of chicken soup, called my drug dealer, bought a bunch of dope, did it, did two shows that night and did not eat another bite of food or sleep one minute for six days. I did two shows a night. Did not sleep one minute or eat one mouthful for six days. I lost 17 pounds. You should have seen me. I looked like a dead man. I nearly fell asleep in the middle of songs. The whole week I stayed in that suite, played gin rummy with my drug dealer for 12, 15 hours at a time, and snorted dope.

I stopped doing cocaine long enough to take a Valium to get me calm enough to sing. Then as soon as the show was over, I'd start right back again, same deal.

I had promised my friend Darryl Royal that I would stop doing drugs. He went on a little trip with me down to North Carolina and we went on a walk and he said, "You have to stop." And I said, "Okay, I can do this on my own, and if I can't quit, I'll go with you," because he wanted to take me to a treatment center in California. I said, "I'll make you a deal: I can do this, Darryl." And he said, "No, you can't."

I did pretty good for 17 days without the cocaine. Then I went to Fort Worth and my disease began to talk to me. I saw this guy that I had known for a while—he's a drug dealer—and my disease said, *You've been a good guy. You've really been so good. I'm so proud of you. Just do one gram. Just have some fun tonight. You're in Fort Worth, at Billy Bob's. Let it go.* So I did and it turned into a three-day binge.

Later that month in Dallas, there was another three-day binge. It was the first time I ever freebased cocaine. I did it for three days with some very close friends of mine I'd known for two hours. I finally wound up crawling on the floor picking lint out of the carpet to put in the freebase pipe. I crawled into the bathroom of the hotel. Everybody had left because we'd run out of drugs. I looked in the mirror and saw this very sick, tired, lonely, hopeless, helpless human being and I said, "God, if you don't help me, I'm going to die."

I got up somehow, God help me. Got to the airport. I had to talk the cab driver into giving me his address because I had no money to pay the $30 cab ride. As I tried to get out of the car, as fate would have it, or as God would have it, I saw a friend named Michael. Michael was, at the time, the bartender at the Admiral's Club for American Airlines. He'd seen me drunk and ripped, and had served me booze for years. He saw that I was in pretty rough shape. He paid the cab driver, got me to the Admiral's Club, called my wife and told her that he was putting me on a plane. I was absolutely insane, nuts. I'd been freebasing for three days.

The next day my friend Ron Carpenter, who was a road manager, called me and said, "Larry, let's have lunch," and it was a tone of voice that I never heard Ronnie use. I knew something was wrong. He was either going to leave or quit or something. At that moment it dawned on me in no uncertain terms that I had to come to grips with this situation. I called Darryl. We arranged to meet in Fort Worth three or four days later. I told my wife that I was going to check into a treatment center. She broke down in tears of joy.

I met Darryl in Fort Worth, did a concert—another concert at Billy

Bob's, as luck would have it—flew to California, did Family Feud, got in a limo, went to a Mexican food joint, had a Number One plate with extra chili and four Mexican beers, then got into the limo and went to the treatment center.

I have an addictive personality. I'm a classic type A, balls-to-the-wall guy. I never bought one of anything in my life if I could afford a dozen. I just went to my tailor two months ago—the clothes that I ordered finally came in. I didn't realize that I ordered 11 pairs of pants. I didn't really need 11 pairs of pants, especially three black ones and two more white ones. Just the same, that compulsive attitude is still a part of me. I think from the first I was addicted to the thrill of it. I wanted the fastest car, the prettiest woman, the nicest looking suit—that was my life. I was addicted to the thrill. So the first time I did it, shoot.

The physical addiction probably took a little longer. From the neck up, hell's bells, baby, I was hooked the first time. If I could scream it from the mountaintops I would say, "You do not have to die drunk. You do not have to die loaded. You do not have to die with a needle stuck in your arm. Somewhere there's help." It's not a matter of giving up anything, it's a matter of receiving something. It's like I've heard it said: "Come try our way and if you don't like it, we'll gladly refund you every bit of your misery."

Chapter V

SHOCK THE MONKEY

The fortune teller looked into my eyeballs
Wrinkles on her face about to crack.
"You best believe that you ain't goin' nowhere,
Unless you get that monkey off your back."

—Aerosmith
"Monkey On My Back"

Chances are you've thought about it more than a few times: waking up with a pounding headache, stomach stirring to a possible eruption. You swear you'll never drink again. Sounds good at the time, but most likely you'll gather enough energy to feed your addiction later that night. When we're actively drinking, quitting rarely seems to be the answer. It's an avenue we'd rather ignore when we're using.

The term alcoholic is still very misunderstood. For many, it conjures the image of a bum on the street drinking from a paper bag; or the unshaven man who reaches to turn off the alarm clock, then grabs the open bottle of Scotch for the usual morning burn. It's shameful, pathetic and embarrassing.

Destroy that image.

An alcoholic is a brain surgeon, actor, million-dollar athlete, CEO of a billion-dollar corporation, truck driver, minister, next-door neighbor, teacher, taxicab driver, film director, your best friend or maybe even the person who saves your life. It can be anyone in any occupation. It's certainly nothing of which to be ashamed.

However, the behavior of a practicing alcoholic is shameful and tremendously painful. It hurts people who care for them—the continuous lying, deceitful behavior and the constant greed, sometimes underlying but usually present. The behavior can change; the damage will need time to heal. Many alcoholics must hit bottom before they quit. Rarely have they risen one morning to proclaim they will walk away from liquor.

73

Many were pushed into quitting because someone else in their lives was sick and tired of their conduct; that person sprang into action to straighten them out. Many have had a spiritual experience of some sort shortly before quitting.

There is no standard formula; that would be too easy. It's very different for everyone. By the time we seriously think of quitting on our own, a number of disastrous events have already occurred. Among them might be the loss of a job, the breakup of a relationship, a run-in with the law, embarrassment with family or friends. If you don't have the extra weight of these problems in addition to the uncontrolled addiction, consider yourself lucky. Most of us are carrying around a ton of garbage.

It's hard for teenagers to realize they may have a drinking problem. Millions of them drink to excess on a regular basis. So why do certain people have to quit, while others continue to drink? Because they're alcoholics. It's a disease. It's not their fault that they are diseased, but they are.

It's not going to go away.

Quitting is another way of life. It's a drastic departure from a previous lifestyle, a time to clean house. And change is very difficult for alcoholics, even change for the better. Transformation is essential for a successful recovery. The process of drinking and using are merely methods we use to escape our feelings, to escape reality. When we quit using and drinking, our feelings are real, they stand at attention. There is no ignoring them. No more deluding the emotions.

It can be frightening for some, but once the promise is made to turn your life around and the healing process begins—once you take it seriously and give it everything you've got—you'll discover this inner power that you can't believe. It will take over your mind, your body and your actions, much like the alcohol and drugs did—but this feeling packs ten times the power. It's a power that has always been with you, that you've avoided for a number of years; you never gave it the time and energy to surface. When it does, it will turn the fears you once escaped into strengths. The anger will now be positive energy.

Once you discover this and witness the immediate results, you'll be astounded. I've yet to meet a person whose life hasn't improved dramatically by finding sobriety and following a recovery program. Not one single person. That's not to say sobriety is an art of perfection; far from it. Some of my toughest times were during my first few months of sobriety. But you live with it, accept it, deal with it, face it, and you beat it. You challenge it and you overcome it. Follow the program and you'll discover your own spiritual identity. You now have the power and strength to succeed, achieve and win.

Steven Tyler tried to quit a number of times. When he finally quit, it was the hardest thing he ever did. Parts of my first conversation with him are next.

Doug Fieger went through a chilling journey with his transformation. He was the first person I interviewed on my many trips to California. When we finished, he picked up the phone and called Tony Sales and Anthony Kiedis, suggesting to them that they be in the book. The next day, I talked with both of them. Thanks again, Doug.

Kiedis and I talked at length about his relationship with Hillel Slovak, his best friend who died of a drug overdose in 1988.

Dallas Taylor is a very fortunate man. Several years into his sobriety he nearly lost his life due to earlier excessive drinking.

Nils Lofgren agonized over quitting. His life was a downward spiral until he decided to put everything on the back burner and check into a treatment center. He wasn't sure how his boss would react to his admission of being an alcoholic.

Steven Tyler

Steven Tyler is a recovering alcoholic and drug addict. He's the lead singer and lyricist of Aerosmith.

You have to be careful of the vim and vigor we used to cop our drugs. We used to spend a day to cop and if we got it by the end of the night, we were happy. All of the energy we put out all day long and all of the misery and lies, all of the grief that we put up with to cop those drugs was an insane, intense vim and vigor.

Just snorting a few granules put me in a place where I thought I could—at any time and any given moment—have someone say, "You're on," and it's *The Tonight Show,* and I'd walk out in front of millions of people. I could have done that at any time, or so I thought, with heroin. Come to find out that I feel so good all the time now, much better than I did when I snorted heroin. I never thought that was possible. I used to dream that I found a bag of dope in a wall

76

somewhere or a suitcase full of it so I could do a little bit every day for the rest of my life.

At times I'd have a seizure, wake up, and everyone would say I'd had a seizure. I'd say, "Fuck you, I did not. I don't know what you're talking about." Then I'd sneak off to the bathroom and shoot up another load. That's not the real down at the moment. The real downer is when someone comes around and makes you realize this kind of stuff because you don't realize it. That's why we're called dis-eased. We use despite adverse consequences.

I guess for me it was when the band told me there is no band. That really affected me. In the beginning they pushed me blindly into going to rehab. Only thing they knew was their self-preservation. They were thinking, "Holy shit, this fucking guy's out of his mind. If we don't get him in there, we won't have a band. Our lead singer is crazy. He's nodding out while we're writing songs. If they see him like this we won't get the record deal, so holy shit, we've got to get him in some place."

They did that—on the one hand out of love, on the other out of blind fear, not realizing that they themselves were diseased, too, and were a major reason that we might not get a record contract.

By throwing me in there, little did they know that when I got out, the counselors would say, "You're not going back into that environ-ment. You're going to be using again by the day after tomorrow. So we'll just see you again next month." And I would cry and flip out and say, "Fuck you. You don't have any faith in me. I can do it."

Well, three rehabs later I came to realize that when I got out of there, I had to tell the guys to be strong, that this was no laughing matter. I told them that if they didn't get straight, I wasn't joining them. In doing that, I found out that I could stand there and say, "If we've got the support of each other, we can all be straight."

You have to be careful of the vim and vigor we used to cop our drugs. We used to spend a day to cop and if we got it by the end of the night, we were happy. All of the energy we put out all day long and all of the misery and lies, all of the grief that we put up with to cop those drugs was an insane, intense vim and vigor.

What we're doing now is experiencing the same thing without the drugs. It's like the horse running the extra mile without the carrot in front of him. The drugs have been replaced. What we see now is a big, beautiful picture of ourselves—there's a gratitude bag there. In it is a picture of Jesus, or whoever we choose as our higher power—and a picture of ourselves and all that neat stuff.

When we're on the road, kids from some of the local rehabs will stop by backstage to talk for a while. I still really get a lot out of relating to strangers on that level. It's something that I never had in rock 'n' roll, even though people think you do—you're a big star in their eyes, but when you get to town, what do you really have to relate to them? You sign an autograph and say good-bye. But with these kids, we can really relate because we've been through the same pain together.

I'm a teenager at heart and when someone says, "Don't go in there," that's the door I go in. You tell kids, "Don't do it, just say no to drugs." That's bullshit. That's like saying, "Cheer up," to a manic-depressive.

Success was a long time coming. That has allowed me to look at my sobriety as the miraculous thing that it is, and therefore something to be treated with great respect. Otherwise the flower will wither and die in my hands. The worst thing for people tending their garden is to watch drought come and kill it right in front of their eyes. We have to be real careful with it.

One of the greatest things I've learned from treatment is that I can walk away when someone has drugs. I can just turn around and walk out the door. Go as fast as I can because this disease that is in all of us will eventually win us over. That motherfucker will say, "Hey, there's a reason to stay. Why don't you just leave him your phone number for later." So when I turn around and walk out, I know that it's over.

Sobriety allows us to really work on the music. I stuck around after the sessions (on *Pump*). I just believe that if you want to do something and make it really great, just walk an extra mile no matter what. So when the day was over, I'd listen to the stuff again or stick around for an extra hour or two after everyone left, just to fuck around with the vocals and tracks. I did a lot of crazy things and said, "Why not, let's use it"—like the beginning of "Elevator," the beginning of "Monkey," all kinds of stuff—and I had a lot of fun in the studio doing that.

I've come to the great realization that I work best under pressure. Whether it's fear or whatever the process is, I work best. I hate it. I don't like somebody telling me that I have to do a vocal tomorrow and they're not happy with the first verse and all that. It's rejection, even though it comes from a loving place. When I do my art, I don't judge it from what others think of it, yet I must let their feelings in the door. It's a very hard thing for me to deal with at the time. I want to say, "Fuck you. I'm the artist." Then I want to say, "Well, Jesus, if I don't ask for help, I won't get anywhere." I have to be discreet and learn it. It's the better part of my career right now, learning and taking direction from people not in the picture frame. I'm in the picture frame. If you want to buy a piece of art, you have to stand back and look at it. I can't even leave the canvas sometimes.

Sometimes I have the insight to go out of it. I'm more open to those people. To be creative and to open my Pandora's box sometimes means for me to be an asshole. It's difficult at times, writing an album, yet—short of some of my experiences in rehab—I've never had better times.

Doug Fieger

Doug Fieger is a recovering alcoholic and drug addict. He's the lead singer of The Knack, whose first album sold more than seven million copies, producing the smash hit "My Sharona." He was propelled from struggling artist to superstar within a few weeks. Currently, Doug is working on a follow-up to the band's greatest hits collection, in addition to appearing as one of Dan Conner's poker playing buddies on *Roseanne*.

What I heard at this meeting
was that I wasn't crazy, but that
I had a disease. See, I just thought I was
insane. It really clicked and it made
very good sense to me that I had
a disease I couldn't control. I was
being reborn. I didn't know that.
I thought I was dying.

I got sober a year and nine months after the band broke up. During that year and a half, I was pretty well out of my mind all the time. I'd come to at about one o'clock in the afternoon and *The Rockford Files,* which was my favorite television show, would be on at two. I'd get up around one-thirty and brush my teeth. I'd go make myself a tall boy of vodka and pink lemonade, and I'd sit at the edge of the bed and watch *The Rockford Files.* Halfway through the show I'd make myself another drink and then I'd get into the shower, then take telephone calls and get myself ready to go out and get high that night—get together with friends and get high, go to a club. That was basically my day. I did that until I passed out, or I'd keep going and do a couple of days, then I'd die for a day. That was my life.

I used to drive with one hand over my eye because I would see quadruple lanes. I'll never forget driving from St. Tropez to Monte Carlo. In France you can drive 120 miles per hour if you want to, and I was driving that fast. I had never driven that road before in my life. I was completely out of my mind. I'm driving with one hand over my eyes because where there's two lanes I'm seeing four.

I used to drive around L.A. with an open thing of amyl nitrate between my knees. I was like the guy in *Blue Velvet.* You know that guy? I'd pick it up, and I'd be driving and I'd go [inhales]. I mean, there must be a God because I didn't die and I didn't kill anybody else.

I always took a lot of drugs. The only thing that increased with stardom was my ability to afford them. But I got as high as I could get from the time that I was 13, 14, until I couldn't get high anymore, until I had to stop. At various times in my life I would befriend dealers and whenever that happened, I got as high as I could possibly get. It really wasn't that success caused me to use drugs more; I was a confirmed drug addict from the get-go.

What I wanted to do was get high. That was my primary purpose. I loved doing other things that I did and I'm a little bit amazed at what I accomplished being as high as I was. It's surprising. But even before that, when I was a little kid, I'd make model cars and airplanes, army tanks, whatever, and I'd always sniff the glue. I used to like to hold my breath until I passed out.

When we were very young, my parents would give us wine coolers. They'd fill a glass half full with red wine and put ginger ale in. They were hoping that if we were running around being rambunctious at a grown-up party, they'd give us one of those and we'd go to sleep. Well, I'd come back for three or four more.

I went with my grandmother on a trip to Norway when I was 14. You could drink there at any age as long as you could put the money on the table. I was drunk pretty much the whole trip. Every time we'd go into a restaurant that had a bar, I'd have a beer or a couple of them. The beer over there was more alcoholic, so I'd get really looped, but I could hold my liquor well—really, really well for a slight skinny guy.

I totaled my car one time. I was completely drunk and driving in Hollywood and hit a divot in the road, one of those rain divots that they have here for runoff. My car was so low that the front of it hit the other side of the divot and it went up in the air. It was a Porsche. I was going 30 miles per hour and the car went up in the air. Reflexively I turned the wheel to the right. When I came down, my tires were pointed to the right and I ran right under a parked car. My car was like a sardine can someone had opened up to the windshield.

Everybody came out of their houses shouting, "Are you all right?" I didn't do any damage to the other car, one of those old Oldsmobiles. My car had $25,000 worth of damage to it. This guy came running out and asked me if I was all right and I said, "Yeah, but I need a drink." So he took me up to his apartment and he poured me a small shot of vodka. I swallowed it, then I took the bottle and drank that. God, I'm amazed I didn't die.

I was at a friend's house with a couple of using buddies watching fights, and we started drinking. We went out to get some more coke and stopped off to buy another bottle of vodka. One of the guys was dealing at the time, so we must have done five, maybe six, grams and a couple bottles of vodka. By the end of the evening we got into a fistfight. It was probably one in the morning when I got home to this new house I had in Benedict Canyon. My wife was there with an old girlfriend of mine. I was very abusive and was screaming and wasn't feeling very well because I got into a fistfight with this guy. I went upstairs and took a bath.

I remember lighting all these candles and I thought—I can't remember exactly why the thought came into my head—of the Roman Emperors. This is funny; I don't think I've ever told this story before. I was going to slit my wrists like the old Roman Emperors. I was feeling misunderstood or something. So I lit all these candles and got the only straight razor blade in the house, one I'd been using to cut up cocaine for the past three months. It was pretty dull. I got into the bathtub and started hacking away at my wrists with this razor blade. After a couple of times I said, "Ow, that hurts." It just didn't do anything. It didn't cut the skin. It just hurt. I'm lying there in the tub, I've got all these candles lit around me and suddenly I was above myself. I was looking down at this scene and I was in my body and I was out of my body at the very same time. I heard a voice say very clearly, "Doug, you're a very sick boy and you need help." I heard this voice as clearly as I would hear yours if you said it to me.

I got out of the bathtub; I didn't even dry myself off. I pulled on a pair of pants, put on a sweatshirt—I think one of my wife's sweatshirts—inside out. I pulled on these pink boots I had and walked down the stairs. I heard this voice come out of my mouth and it said, "Doug, you're a very sick boy and you need help." They looked at me and said, "Do you want to go to the hospital?" and I said, "Yes, I'd like to go to the hospital. I'm not feeling well."

So they drove me to Cedars-Sinai emergency room. I thought I was going to get checked into the hospital and sleep it off, but the next thing I knew, there were these four big guys around me strapping me down to this table. They took me off to St. John's Mental Hospital, where I spent the better part of a month. That's the last time I got high.

The first day I kind of came to. I was locked in a ward that looked like *One Flew Over the Cuckoo's Nest*. There were a number of people in there. One guy was talking to the wall—I'll never forget that—and another guy was carrying everything he owned with him all the time, running up and down the halls. I was put in a room with a guy who wore slippers; he'd take them off and put his shoes on when he went to bed. When my wife came to visit me, she freaked out.

She had gone home to sleep after dropping me off, and when she came back, she saw me in that ward. She told the nurses, "I'm pulling him out of here unless you put him in a ward that isn't like this. Put him in with normal people because he ain't crazy like this," even though I really was. I mean, I was hearing things and I was watching guys talk to the walls and I thought, *Yeah, you know, I can relate*, because I'd been psychotic for a good long while and didn't even know it. I was functioning in the world, but I was pretty much out of my mind. It was drug-induced psychosis, cocaine psychosis most particularly, and alcohol.

I would get really high and really paranoid or I would accuse somebody of doing something—looking at me the wrong way, stuff like that. That regularly happened, but I felt normal. I felt like I was at home in this place, but they moved me to this private room on another ward, and basically they just left me alone.

There was a woman in there who was two years sober. She had been attacked and it traumatized her, so she committed herself. She could come and go as she pleased. We'd stay up late at night and talk. One night she asked me, "Are you an alcoholic?" And I said, "No, look at me. Do I look like an alcoholic?" And she said, "Well, I am." She was really beautiful. She seemed really together. I didn't know what the hell she was doing there. I thought she was a spy. I had no idea. She said, "Well, I'm an alcoholic and I go to these meetings. If you ever want to go, just tell me." I got so bored after being there for about two-and-a-half weeks that I asked her to take me to a meeting.

What I heard at this meeting was that I wasn't crazy, but that I had a disease. I heard it; it's like I got it. I heard that I wasn't insane. See, I just thought I was insane. It really clicked and it made very good sense to me that I had a disease I couldn't control. My life as I knew it was over. I was being reborn. I didn't know that. I thought I was dying. But my life was over and that's the sense I had.

I have a very difficult time with change, even change for the better. It's like the story of what happens if you take a child and put him in a closet—you lock him in a closet for the first three or four years of his life—and then you take him out into the beautiful meadow. The sun's shining, it's a glorious day, everything is beautiful, and you have this three-by-three cardboard box in the middle of the field. He'll get into the cardboard box and close it off because he feels much more comfortable locked inside a cardboard box than he does out in a beautiful meadow. That's the kind of guy I was. I was the boy in the cardboard box. Suddenly I was in this beautiful meadow and I didn't know what to do with it. It was very uncomfortable.

I had no choice, though; I couldn't die. And it wasn't that I thought I was indestructible because I knew sooner or later I would die, but I couldn't go and get a gun and blow my brains out. I tried to run my car into trees many, many times. As a matter of fact, the night I was also trying to slit my wrists with this razor blade that was so dull it wouldn't cut me—Emperor Caligula here—I was trying to crash this brand new Corvette I bought. I thought, I'll buy a Corvette, that'll fix it. I was trying to drive it into a tree, but I couldn't do it.

I describe a lot of my last years drinking and using like this: being on a speeding train at night—pitch black night—riding through the country where there's no street lights and there's a storm going on outside, a very violent storm. Every once in a while there's a flash of lightning and it wakes you up. You look out the window and see the world illuminated by this flash of lightning. You see the rain pouring down, and there's a fierce wind. Then you go back to sleep. That's what my life was like for the last two-and-a-half years of drinking and using. I had this flash of images, and everything filtered through some kind of madness—drunken madness or heroin madness or cocaine madness or combinations of all of them.

I have a friend named Tony who says, "All we've got is today. All I have is Thursday, that's all I've got." I've got this moment, talking, listening, hearing, experiencing, smelling, tasting, and it's tough because we have brains that can create cities in the air. The challenge for me is to keep pulling that back. I meditate every day and I'm constantly trying to keep a conscious contact with a power far greater than myself. It is being here, now. That's what it is for me.

I just want a gentle confirmation, moment by moment, that I'm part of the real flow, part of the whole, and that's a second at a time. Today I'm talking with you, if I get a chance I'll go and work out. I'm going to the MTV Awards tonight. That's my day. That's as much as I've planned. Of course, I've planned other things in my week and I have things planned for my future, for the next month, but I don't know what's going to happen. I may walk out of the house and a plane could have dropped a safe or a bit of frozen waste and it may hit me on the head while I'm walking down Melrose: you can never tell. So I try just to be here. It's a lot more rewarding. I'm having a wonderful time.

I'm always struck by the truth of the paradoxes of recovery. You've got to let it go in order to keep it; surrender in order to win; give in order to receive. All great philosophies have taught these things since the beginning. It's just that alcoholics need it spelled out a little more particularly.

We share the same kind of camaraderie and elation that the survivors of a shipwreck must feel when they're in the lifeboat watching the Titanic go down. There's this amazing sense that we survived this together and we all experienced roughly the same thing. Some person may have escaped from the cabin on the port deck and another one was aft, but pretty much everybody was in the same boat. We all got out and now we're in this little life raft, and we're still alive.

Anthony Kiedis

Anthony Kiedis is a recovering alcoholic and drug addict. He's the lead singer of the Red Hot Chili Peppers. The band's original guitarist, and Anthony's best friend, Hillel Slovak died of a drug overdose in 1988.

*It's so lonely when you don't
even know yourself*

"Knock Me Down"
—Red Hot Chili Peppers

The band had just arrived in England from America. I had begun the journey of becoming a cleanster by then. I was still unsuccessful in my attempt to stay clean, but I had been exposed to the concepts of recovery. I knew that there was a way to live my life without having to rely on drugs and alcohol.

Even though I was still using, because I had this little glimpse of enlightenment I was able to see that it wasn't necessary, and that there was a viable fellowship and a viable program I could be a part of that would allow me not to have to live that way any longer.

We went to England and Hillel was still using pretty heavily. He got into a fairly serious withdrawal because he decided that he was going to try to kick his heroin habit. I was explaining to him that it was essential for us both to get off drugs if we wanted to continue sharing our lives and making music together. We had pretty much exhausted all the years of using; it had become nothing but detrimental to our lives and our careers. I'm not saying that I regret all of the experiences of being high in my lifetime because that was part of my life. I just have to accept it that way.

I saw him resisting my effort to talk him into going to the next step of life, which for us was leaving drug addiction behind and moving off into a whole new realm of cleansterism. He was resisting. I was thinking: *This person needs to get knocked off his pedestal of beliefs because it's going to be damaging to him in the long run if somebody doesn't just basically kick his ass and tell him what time it is.*

We went into his room at the hotel to kick, and that's when I wrote the concept for "Knock Me Down" in my notebook. It just dawned on me that that's really what it was about for him. He was thinking he was immortal and untouchable by life's destructive forces. He had this image in his mind of, *If Jimmy Page can do it and still be alive and still play guitar today, then why can't I?* It wasn't quite that literal, but this was an underlying sensation that I know he had been feeling for many years. That's when the song was born.

I came back to L.A. and I kind of forgot about the tune until Hillel died. I wasn't really into writing about his death at that point because I hadn't dealt with it myself on a personal level. I wasn't ready to get these ideas out and write about them. Then John, our new guitar player, was looking at these lyrics and said, "These are some seriously honest lyrics. I think you should expand on this." He had a melodic structure for a tune all written out, and I just sat there and I started scratching out the rest of the lyrics to the tune. There's that very last thing—*It's so lonely when you don't even know yourself*—where I tried to put myself in the position of remembering what it was like to feel that way, and to just get very honest about how I felt about Hillel, about how much I missed him, and the very last concept that came to me was *I remember what it was like for myself when I was using.* I would isolate and I would be completely alone. I would have no ability to communicate with people that I loved so I would turn to myself. I was so nebulous in my own being that I couldn't even turn to myself because I was emotionally scattered and fragmented to a point where I didn't even know myself any more. I think that is one of the only ways a human being's brain can operate on a lucid level: to know yourself. When you don't have a friend and you don't even dig hanging out with yourself, it becomes very lonely.

Sometimes I just can't talk about Hillel. Sometimes I just end up a blubbering mess of tears and sadness. Other times I really like talking about it. Hillel was a very special person. He was an amazingly creative man from the time he was around six years old. He was a phenomenal artist in many forms—drawing, painting—and one of the most original and unique guitar players I've ever heard. He was just a ridiculously sensitive, creative, loving human being that had this hole in his soul that he didn't know how to fill. He had this void. You could see it in his face. Here's this person that you just want to hug constantly because he had that kind of energy about him. You wanted to hold him and you wanted to love him, you wanted to spend time laughing with this person. But he had a visible sadness about him. We were best friends throughout our teens and we just had a nonstop joy ride of fun, whether it was driving his car through the rain in the hills, listening to music or just stopping and looking at the city lights in the rain—you know, talking about giving girls head in the back of his Datsun and stuff like that. Then gradually that hole became more mature and more visible. You would look at this guy and you knew he had a weird sadness.

He never had a relationship with his father, which I know fucked him up. He dealt with the pain that manifested because of that hole by using heroin. When he found heroin, that filled the hole. He thought he had found a valuable friend with heroin. What his sadness was, I'll never exactly know, but heroin defused that sadness.

Without you realizing what's happening, heroin sucks the love out of you. The love of life, the love of people, the love of music, the love of whatever it is that you have a love for. It's very deceiving because it'll numb a pain, but it'll numb your love as well. It'll numb your joy and your fervor to discover what it is in life that you were meant to explore.

It kills you, too. Eventually you either die or you end up in a puddle of trouble in the street. You end up in prison or you end up in a loony bin. Hillel could not fathom the concept that there was anything else in life that could deal with that hole except for heroin. We were very close, though when we used drugs, we didn't use them together. We didn't communicate frequently because we were both off in our own individual worlds of drug use. Maybe we were so embarrassed and ashamed of these worlds. Maybe we didn't want to expose them to each other even though we each knew thoroughly what the other was up to.

I was always the one people said would die. I was always the obviously out-of-control person using. Hillel seemed to have it under control. He was very much more orderly about it. He didn't seem to have the sort of death-wish binges that I would go on. He stayed in his apartment and hid behind his drugs. He didn't deal with people too much. He had his cat. He couldn't really seem to find a girl to spend his life with, which was part of his sadness. Drugs don't make that any easier. But everyone always kind of assumed that I would kick the bucket, that Hillel would go on. It was really only me that saw how deep he was getting into it.

At the same time, I was struggling with getting clean because I had been enlightened by the awareness of recovery. It was a very strange thing. I went to meetings and I knew they were the answer. I knew they didn't want anything from me. I knew it wasn't a religion, that it was just addicts helping other addicts. I filtered everything that I learned from the program to Hillel. I would drag him to a meeting here, a meeting there, but then I'd go get high and he'd get high. I think in the back of his mind he knew that it was a possible solution, but he didn't want a solution.

When he died I refused for about a week to believe or accept it in any way whatsoever. I stayed high. My girlfriend was just bawling her eyes out. I came home at about six in the morning. I had been out all night and she told me that Hillel was dead. She was screaming and crying and I was just like, "Shut up. What are you saying that for? It's not funny. Don't tell me that." I could not register it. When I finally realized that he was dead, I ignored it for probably a month. I didn't allow myself to think about it. I had an uncanny ability to avoid the issue. In my heart and soul I just wouldn't face it.

I started using again right after he died. I didn't know how to face reality without the emotional cushion of drugs. I just had never learned. I started using drugs on a regular basis at the age of 11. I just never went through the face-to-face experience of learning to cope with life. The worst thing that's ever happened to me was Hillel dying. To face that was an impossibility for me at the time, so I went back to using. It was the ultimate misery, just feeling like I was going to spontaneously combust at any moment. I was forcing so much grief back inside me that there just wasn't any more room for grief. It was like I had a giant fireman's hose shooting grief down my throat. I was just going to explode because I wouldn't take my mouth off the nozzle. I didn't sleep for a week. I put somewhere between 50 and 100 puncture marks into my arm. I was just over the edge. I don't want to give the impression that that's what it takes to get you to the point where you have to be clean, but that's what it took for me. It was a bad week. It was a real bad week.

I would not face Hillel's death until I went to the hospital, and even then I was so closed down from drugs that I never cried and never thought about it. A friend of mine came to the hospital and said, "I'm going to take you up to where Hillel's buried." We went up to the grave. I felt real uncomfortable. I wasn't feeling a damn thing. I felt stone cold. I was sitting there and thought, "Well, I don't know what you want from me. This doesn't really do anything." And he said, "Let me leave you alone here for a minute." And he walked away. I just started talking to Hillel, who I knew as Slim, and I said, "You know, Slim . . ." and all of a sudden for the next hour I became a faucet of tears and snot. It was pouring out of my head like it was all I was made of.

Obviously my friend knew that was in there. He knew that I had to get it out. From that point on I've been able to deal with this death to a certain degree. He also suggested that I make a deal with Hillel at that point in time: that if I was ever going to stick a needle in my arm again, I would come back to that sight and say, "Yo, Slim, I'm going to go stick a needle in my arm." It's always worked as a spiritual safeguard against doing that. In a way, I would feel like I was betraying Hillel if I was to go back and use. Whether that's bullshit or not, if it keeps me clean, I'm willing to accept it.

I deal with things a lot better now. I accept people a lot more. When I was using, I felt as though people had to be how I wanted them to be, and if they weren't, they were wrong. That was just one of the character defects that went along with alcoholism. When you get clean, you become aware of the things that you've always tried to resolve in the past. I'm not saying I deal with them that much better, but at least because I'm aware of them I have a chance to deal with them. If I'm being hypercritical of another person with whom I have a relationship, I have the sense to know what I'm doing. I have the opportunity to correct it, whereas before I didn't even realize it was a character defect.

Relationships are better, for one thing. The sex is so much better, the love is so much more pure. I'm not so self-centered. Before, when I'd be in a relationship with a girl, if she wasn't using, she had to deal with this person that was going to go away for the entire night. If she was lucky, I'd come back in the morning alive, which basically put her in the state of ultimate anxiety for that entire period of time because her loved one was out on the streets doing God-knows-what to himself, and maybe he'd come back and maybe he'd end up like Hillel. That's what my old girlfriend was going through because she never knew if I was going to come back. She was just torn to shreds for the period of time we were together. Now I don't cause people that sort of anxiety. I don't put people through the emotional meat grinder I used to. It wasn't an intentional thing; it was an inadvertent by-product of my self-centered lifestyle. I didn't consciously say, *Okay, I'm going to absolutely mutilate this person's emotional life because of what I want to do.* I loved them, they loved me, but I had a need to do drugs constantly. I didn't stop to think what that was going to do to them. I was probably a pretty tremendous asshole a lot of the time.

I've always considered myself some sort of fantastic explorer of the world's gifts, but when I was using I didn't see anything. I wasted my entire day getting money together, copping, thinking about it, nodding out, falling asleep, being sick—it was ridiculous. Ninety percent of the things that I do in my life, 90 percent of the things I love to do—making music, writing songs, skydiving, having sex, swimming in my pool, hiking through the mountains, traveling the world, being successful in my band—did not happen when I was using. You ask yourself why anybody would give up so much and how does anybody get that deep into it? But for me it was a remarkably deceptive and gradual process of just being really very naive about drug addiction.

When you start off using drugs as a teenager, you don't think of the term drug addiction; you think of partying, of having a great time doing something rebellious. I believe that rebellion is an essential and healthy part of growing up, but to do it in a self-destructive manner defeats the entire purpose. If you want to rebel against your parents, do it without hurting yourself. Do it without destroying your opportunities and your feelings and your love. For me it was just a gradual erosion of my love, my love for everything from human beings to the planet to the animals on the planet. All of my love was slowly eroded because everything was replaced over a ten-year period with only one thing: using.

I think only you can make the final decision to quit. I couldn't have done it without the wisdom, the experience, strength and hope of the fellowship, specifically of certain fellows in that fellowship. It's another cliché, but it rings true for me: it's an inside job. You have to turn it over from the inside out and make that commitment. It's a combination of enough elements that have to happen at the same time, I suppose. You have to be despondent enough to be willing to try something completely new that your brain wouldn't have otherwise allowed you to experiment with because you had too much pride, or you wanted to do it your way. I love the expression I hear at meetings all the time, that people feel like the cosmic piece of shit that the universe revolves around. I can relate to that so much because having the disease of alcoholism is a very mysterious combination of massive insecurity and massive egomaniacal activity at the same time. It's an egomaniac with an insecurity complex. That's how I feel a lot of the time.

You have all these preconceptions and previous ways of dealing with your problems. You get to a point where it just isn't happening. Then you become willing. I had to go through what I had to go through to get to that point. Even during the last year of going in and out, I knew it was up. I knew I was destined for being clean. It was only a matter of time. I really hadn't faced the fact that I wasn't a perfect being yet. I was still holding onto the idea of not needing anybody's help and doing it on my own one more time.

I know the importance of meetings. I can be depressed and slipping back into my old "why me?" thinking and this great wave of loneliness we all get caught up in. And I'll allow myself to be taken away by this wave of loneliness and just kind of dwell in it. Then I go to a meeting and I say, *What the hell am I thinking? I've been given a second chance to a wonderful life on this planet with my friends. Why don't I just realize all of the things that have been given to me in the last few years and focus on that instead of the fact that maybe the world isn't the way I want it to be.* Meetings have the uncanny ability to take me out of my bullshit and put me into a fun place, a fun state of mind. I've made some of the greatest friends of my life at meetings and I hear the greatest pieces of wisdom there.

Not going to meetings is probably the most common denominator for people who relapse. *Why did you relapse? Well, I stopped going to meetings.* I don't know what it is about them. I don't even think it's necessary for me to question their importance. I heard that if I keep going to meetings I won't go back to that life I used to lead. I think it's essential that you go to meetings for another purpose, which is to keep in touch with where you came from. To me, that is probably one of the single most powerful aspects of the program, that it's a perpetual program. People are given a life, a clean life, and once they get to a certain point for their own selfish purposes of keeping what they've found, they are obligated to go out to the newcomer and give to him what they have been given in the program. By doing that you see where you came from. It's like a dual purpose of showing somebody with some time where they came from, and that person is able to give experience, strength and hope to this newcomer. It just seems like the perfect arrangement of perpetual motion for a fellowship to have that element. The idea of one addict helping another, there is nothing that touches that as far as I'm concerned. I'm not going to listen to a doctor, to a psychologist, to a psychiatrist, to a family member who is not an addict. Nobody knows the life of an addict except for another addict, and the only place where you'll be with other addicts that are recovering and talking about recovering is in the meetings.

My way of looking at Hillel's death is really less that he died of heroin than he died of the disease of alcoholism. When I picture him dead, I don't picture him dead because he poisoned himself, but because he had the disease of addiction, the disease of alcoholism, which is the disease of loneliness. He was so fucking lonely that he died. That's how I feel about it. Technically and specifically he died from taking too many drugs, but why did he take too many drugs? Because he was so fucking lonely. I never really got too heavily into the coroner's report, but there were a number of chemicals in his body that caused him to die and they weren't all heroin. Heroin was just sort of the brunt of the poisoning blow. Heroin collapses your lungs if you take too much of it, for whatever reason I'm not sure. Your lungs collapse and they freeze together like sucking the air out of a bag. You're so incredibly unaware under the influence of heroin that you just kind of fall asleep. It's a combination of falling asleep and not breathing. You pass out, your lungs pass out, your brain and your lungs pass out together.

Usually if you pass out at least you keep breathing because your lungs are still there, or if your lungs collapse and you're awake you can force yourself to breath, but when you pass out and your lungs collapse at the same time, you don't get any oxygen to the brain.

He died alone in his house, which is really one of the saddest parts about the whole deal. He wasn't just some drug addict out there with a bunch of other drug addicts getting high—he was alone in his house. If he wasn't so lonely and wasn't so into isolating—just being by himself, dwelling in the sadness of being so lonely—I would have been there or some girl would have been there or somebody else would have been there, and he wouldn't have died because it's not that hard to save somebody when they OD on heroin. But he was alone except for his cat. That was the animal he could most relate to at that point. He just wasn't able to relate to people well enough to give that love away, so he gave it to this cat he really loved. Terrible thing. It's really a terrible thing.

Dallas Taylor

Dallas Taylor is a recovering alcoholic and drug addict. He's the former drummer for Crosby, Stills, Nash & Young and performed session and live work with Jimi Hendrix, Janis Joplin and Jim Morrison. He's now a substance abuse counselor for a Southern California treatment center.

It's unbelievable how my life has transformed. I was not lovable as an addict, not even likable. I was charming. I could charm you if you had something I wanted. I could get you to like me, but it was all manipulation. None of it was real.

I was at the end of a very long bottom. I hadn't really worked as a musician for quite some time.

It seemed every project I'd get involved with would somehow fall apart. I was living in a dingy little place with my now ex-wife. Neither of us was very happy with each other. We were both using.

I was involved with a manager who was also a coke dealer; that's where my sights were. I was still riding the game of my past achievements to get my drugs.

My sole purpose in life was to get drugs and try to maintain that on a daily basis. I was suicidal; I didn't really have much hope for anything. I was angry, really angry, and blaming. I blamed a lot of people for my demise, including my ex-band members and friends. Everybody but me. Taking no responsibility and blaming everyone. Blaming the world for my problems.

One night I got really drunk with my father-in-law and I'd based a little cocaine. I ended up in a blackout. I don't remember a lot of it. What I do remember was a moment of clarity. As loaded as I was, all of a sudden I was very sober. It was like looking out, being someone else looking at me. For the first time in years I really saw what I had become—a pathetic, hopeless drug addict. No longer Dallas Taylor the drummer, the rock star, but this pathetic drug addict.

Then very calmly and very precisely, very methodically, I walked home. For some reason I took my wallet out and threw it. It landed in someone's car. I later got it back from the police station. Took my keys and threw them as far as I could and walked back. I somehow stumbled back to this place I lived in, went directly to the kitchen, pulled out a butcher knife and stabbed myself in the stomach, hari-kiri style. I had attempted suicide many times before—some for attention, some seriously. I think I'd been attempting suicide covertly most of my using life because I'd always put myself in a dangerous situation, whether I was driving too fast, too loaded, owing the wrong dealer, having guns pointed at me, being shot at.

I remember stabbing myself, and my wife (at the time) heard the commotion and walked in. I said, "If I'm alive in the morning, maybe you should take me to the hospital." She said, "Okay," and went to bed. That was pretty much where we had ended. My relationships with everyone had ended. I had alienated everyone.

I did wake up the next morning, in a great deal of pain, and finally tracked my wife down. She wasn't there when I woke up. She had left. She came back and took me to the hospital. I spent about three weeks recovering from the knife wound.

The doctors who took the X rays and explored the wound said it looked as though a surgeon had done it because I had miraculously missed every major organ and artery in that area. It was just a pretty vital area to be sticking stuff into. That was one of the first times I had awareness that *this might be a miracle,* but I wouldn't say that out loud. I wouldn't let anybody hear me say that. I went ahead and they detoxed me. I don't know what happened at what point, but I think I was just too weak, too tired and too beat to fight anymore. I'd like to be able to say I woke up and decided being sober was the greatest thing in the world, but that's just not the case. I fought it all the way. I was in detox for almost two weeks. It was a rough detox. I was hallucinating. They had me all drugged up. I was really out of it. They threatened to send me to a mental hospital on several occasions because I wouldn't allow anybody near me. I was very hostile, a real danger to myself and others. For some reason they didn't send me out. They just worked with me and finally took the medications away.

I remember that first day I woke up and it had been 24 hours since I'd had anything. There was something different about it. First of all, I don't think I'd gone 24 hours in the last 20 years without putting something in my body, even if it was just a beer. There was something very different about it. I remember feeling like a kid, feeling, *Wow, this is great! I don't feel bad. I feel pretty good. Everything looks fresh.* The honeymoon was on. I decided that I really didn't have anywhere else to go. I really had nothing to lose so I figured, *Fuck it, I'll just try it.* I knew at that point I could always go back. Somebody had said to me, "Listen, just give it a try; we'll gladly refund your misery if you don't like it," and that stuck.

I began going to meetings. I remember feeling this tremendous energy. It was like the room was charged with all this energy and I thought, *Wow, this is really cool, you know, people my age and people younger.* They were happy and laughing. I thought, *Maybe I can do this.* That's pretty much what happened.

My first year was tough, though. After I got out of the hospital I had to deal with reality, and reality for me was pretty fucked up. I was in a relationship and a marriage that was based on drinking and using. There was a lot of wreckage in my life.

I didn't have any other skills outside of music, and nobody was willing to give me a shot at playing the drums anymore. They had heard it a million times: "I'm sober, I really am. I've really got it together." They'd trust me and I'd blow it. This happened time after time, and people finally stopped returning my phone calls. So basically I needed a job, and a good friend of mine—this old saxophone player and junkie who had been sober for ten years—said, "Dallas, you need to go to work. You got two choices. I can get you a job at Pizza Hut or you can go work in recovery." Neither one sounded too glamorous. I picked the lesser of the two, which is working in recovery.

What I discovered was that I really enjoy working with the kids. I had an edge on most people because I played at Woodstock. I played with Jimi Hendrix, hung out with Jim Morrison. All these famous dead people, and I'm one of the few who survived. All those drummers and guitar players and singers—friends of mine—are dead from alcohol and drugs.

So I ended up telling my story. Telling kids stories about what it was like to hang out with Hendrix and Morrison and Joplin. Kids liked me and I started to see real results. As a matter of fact, that's how I met my wife. She was a therapist at the hospital I was working at and she noticed I was having this effect on kids.

Just when it looked like everything was going to be okay in my life, I got real sick. I was remarried to someone I love and was very comfortable. I started to get my life back. Then I was told I had end-stage liver disease, which means cirrhosis of the liver—your liver is damaged beyond repair. Basically it's a death sentence. I was told I would die without a liver transplant.

What happened to me, I think, has scared a lot of people because I didn't have this problem at the height of my drinking. It came on after I had five years of sobriety, so people thought it could happen to them also. Crosby, Stills, Nash & Young did a benefit for me and all of a sudden there's a lot of publicity about it. I remember speaking at meetings where I saw people who were visibly scared.

It's like, you know, it can be too late. You can wait too long, and that's part of my pitch when I talk to kids. One of them will say, "Yeah, but you're an old dude, man. You partied and it's all over for you, but I can keep doing it." Well, they diagnosed me with liver damage when I was 21 years old. They said I wouldn't live to be 25. That never stopped me from drinking and using. Once I passed 25, then I knew that they were full of shit and I really went for it. It really was a shock to have five years sober and what appeared to be my life back, and to all of a sudden get this death sentence. It was scary.

The symptoms were subtle at first. The liver is, of course, one of the more vital organs. It's responsible for your blood clotting and for processing food, cleansing your blood, removing toxins from you. As it gets worse, your mental condition gets worse, too.

I was now sober and Eddie Money was one of the guys I auditioned for. It was really a hard thing for me to face because, first of all, I had never auditioned for anyone; but when he called I decided I really wanted to work, so I'd audition. There were several young energetic drummers there and I hadn't played for a while, but I figured what the hell. I remember playing and he pulled me off to the side and said, "Dallas, I don't know what happened to your playing." I couldn't understand what he was talking about. They were all symptoms of my liver damage. Things like that—not being able to play the drums, not being able to sleep, never feeling rested. As a matter of fact, I would always wake up feeling hung over. Always woke up feeling like I'd been on a bender. I couldn't figure that one out. I would hear people talking at meetings about how great they felt after getting sober. They're full of energy and life is wonderful and they're sleeping like babies. I was starting to get really pissed off. I was starting to think, *Well, that's not me. When am I going to start feeling good?* It just kept getting worse.

I ended up getting real sick one night. I had a fever of 107, way past the danger point. I felt like I was going to throw up, but I didn't. I ended up in a hospital and they ran a bunch of tests and said I had internal bleeding. That's when they first discovered it. It was relatively mild compared with how it can be. They pumped me full of blood and released me and then it happened two or three more times. Finally, they called in some experts and ran some more tests and told me I wouldn't make it, that I had six months, maybe a year, unless I had a liver transplant. My liver was damaged beyond repair. Talk about feeling powerless.

I didn't care about living when the doctors told me I wouldn't see 25. I was, *Let's go platinum and die. Fuck this.* But now, for the first time in my life I really wanted to live, and to hear I needed a transplant was really scary.

They handed me this beeper and said, "You're on a list. Go about your life and we'll call you." It was very matter-of-fact for them, but for me it was rough. For Betty, my wife—we'd only been married a year when all this started happening—it looked like everything was going to be cut real short. I also heard stories about people not living long enough for a donor to become available. Time just dragged on. It was six months before they called.

They said once they opened me up and saw it, it looked like a piece of rotten hamburger meat with holes and pits. The timing couldn't have been more perfect because within a matter of a couple weeks I would have been in a coma.

I was really starting to have to walk like I talked. I remember talking to kids about having faith in a higher power, trusting, and that once you get sober everything will be okay. I had to really try and believe that, but it was pretty difficult at times. I'd heard about people who had cancer with no hope, so who's to say there's a higher power? I started really doubting that stuff. But sure enough, it was right on time. Ironically, it was an 18-year-old kid who was killed in an alcohol-related car accident.

Even prior to getting the word, I started learning how to live one day at a time. I was waking up and being truly grateful that I had another day. I started living my life that way. I started working on what's known as acceptance. If I'm meant to live, if I'm meant to receive another miracle in my life, it'll happen. I'd already received plenty. I had five years of sobriety I didn't expect. Had I not become sober, I would have been dead anyway. The fact that I survived the suicide attempt, the fact that I had five years clean and sober, were miracles. I know there are reasons for everything that happens.

Before sobriety, all of my relationships were just superficial, bullshit relationships surrounding drugs. Today, I have friends I can call at three in the morning if I'm in trouble. When I went into surgery, my room was filled with flowers and there was a vigil of 30, 40, 50 people in the waiting room holding meetings while I was in surgery.

It's unbelievable how my life has transformed. I was not lovable as an addict, not even likable. I *was* charming. I could charm you if you had something I wanted. I could get you to like me, but it was all manipulation. None of it was real. As soon as I got what I wanted I'd be gone. It's nothing short of a miracle that I'm sitting here talking with you. I was absolutely dying. Look at this [he lifts his shirt, revealing a massive scar branching in three directions across his chest and abdomen]. Looks like a Mercedes logo. If you drew the circle you'd have the Mercedes logo [laughs]. World-class.

Nils Lofgren

Nils Lofgren is a recovering alcoholic and drug addict. In addition to a successful solo career and performing on two of Ringo Starr's All-Starr world tours, he reigns as guitarist for Bruce Springsteen's E Street Band.

One day at a time. I can't see doing it any other way because for me the thought of never drinking for the rest of my life was a concept I couldn't grasp. I don't even want to think about whether or not I can grasp it today. I don't have to. I just have to think about today.

If you're an alcoholic, drinking is not hard to do. It's the most natural thing in the world. Once you're addicted, it just goes on forever. Alcohol was my drug of choice. I drank all the time. I loved it; it felt great. I was very healthy and pretty indestructible for many years. After about ten years of drinking heavily, without even realizing it, it began to turn on me.

101

I continued to drink for another ten years and it was basically hell.
I kept thinking, *Tomorrow I'm going to wake up and start drinking
and it will work like it used to.* I thought that was a way of life. It was
legal, after all. I went to business meetings with record company exec-
utives and drank. I drank with guys in the bar where I played.
Drinking was what everybody did. So I thought, *It has to work like it
used to.* I was determined it would work because I thought I needed
it, thought it was as much a part of my life as an arm or a leg. I
thought the courage to go after my dreams came from drinking. I
thought if I could just get the girl of my dreams or the house of my
dreams, whatever—the hit record—then everything would be fine,
then I'd be able to get my act together.

But then I had the girl, I had the nice house and I had an incredible job when I joined The E Street Band in 1984. I found myself
drinking heavily after the *Born in the USA* tour. That's when it hit me
that here I was in this great band, had a beautiful wife, the house, the
car, a demo studio in my home, a lot of nice guitars and amps—and
I was completely miserable. I got scared. I had hit an emotional and
spiritual bottom, and I was falling apart inside.

I had been to a few meetings and seen one of my neighbors there.
My wife, Cis, encouraged me to ask him for help and I did. He took
me to a meeting and I spoke for the first time about my feelings. We
had coffee afterwards with another buddy, and I was sitting there saying, "I'll do the 90/90 and I'll get well." Meanwhile I'm telling them
how miserable I am, how completely miserable, and they're saying,
"Nils, why are you being so hard on yourself? If you're this sick and
you feel this bad, why don't you just get some real inpatient help?" I
said, "Oh no, I might lose my job." They said, "Listen, man, if you
don't get that kind of help, the way you're talking, it sounds like
you're going to lose your job and your wife and your friends anyway."
That night, for the first time, I sat there with my feelings and realized
they were right.

I was beaten. I had quit off and on for years; I quit for two days,
two minutes, two weeks, but it was never comfortable. I always went
back to drinking. I finally decided, with the help and encouragement
of Cis, that I had to get some help. I finally surrendered and called a
treatment center.

I was scared to death, really scared. I'd finally admitted the problem. When I came to the point where I admitted to myself I was that

sick, it was very frightening. There was so much shame involved with it all. That didn't go away for a long time. About three weeks into rehab I started getting a handle on it, stopped feeling so bad about it.

When I reached my bottom, I finally had just a moment of clarity and realized how much I wanted help. I finally channeled all the energy I had put into using, drinking and manipulating my life into recovery. I channeled that energy into trying to just accept that I wanted to get well. Every step of the way, my natural instinct was to fight it, to run. It's like, *Oh my God, they're telling me to get well. Not only do I have to stop drinking and doing drugs, but I have to get in touch with all my feelings: my shame, my anger, my rage, my love, my inadequacies. I have to face them on a daily basis, stone-cold sober at all times, forever.*

Even though I constantly felt like this was too much, it took those 20 years of using and drinking, and the last ten years of hating it, it took those memories to remind me that if I didn't stick this out, what was I going to go back to? I knew what I'd go back to was driving around in a car, drinking and lying to everyone that loved me, not being able to even feel, not being able to have any kind of relationship with people that I loved the most. That's what my life became with booze and drugs. It's still the memory of that incomprehensible demoralization that keeps me trying to put one foot in front of the other and heal.

Once I had made the decision to get help, I was determined to see it through, believing that no matter what the consequences my life depended on it. It was heartwarming and inspiring to me how supportive my family and friends were. Bruce knew that I had been struggling with alcohol. When I told him I had to go and get help, he and the entire band were very supportive. One of the gifts of early sobriety for me was the *Tunnel of Love* tour. It showed me how much better I played with a clear heart and head, and I enjoyed it more than ever. Also, I realized how blessed I was with family and friends who loved and supported me.

I had needed to get to the point where all of a sudden the only important thing was to get well. If everyone else is equally important, you're not going to get well. I didn't. I tried to get well on my own for ten years and juggle it all, and it didn't work for me.

Even more than alcohol, my drug of choice was escape. I was so used to escaping, so used to hiding my feelings and drinking my emotions away. It was simple to escape and to leave my problems and feelings behind. I'd go out and play bars, I played nightclubs. Every night kids came up and said, "Hey, let me buy you a drink. Come on, man, I want to let you know how much I appreciate what you did."

In the beginning, playing was tough, too. It took me about three months to learn to play sober. I used to always have a drink on the amp, my double gin and tonic. In between each song, I took a hit. The first three months it was very uncomfortable, but I was determined. I wanted that. Now, I embrace the clarity: I love it. All of a sudden everything is so real—the notes, the people in my face in this funky little bar.

I love life without alcohol and drugs. The greatest thing I ever did was to go and get help, to ask for help. I feel great about my life and I'm not afraid to make mistakes. I'm starting to learn that facing the truth and being honest in itself is a high. That's a newfound joy for me. I go to meetings and I stay hooked into people who are sober.

Today, I'm doing what I need to do, not only to stay clean and sober, but to try to heal. I didn't get clean and sober just to tell you I am, and be miserable inside. I got clean and sober to hopefully continue to heal. If I'm not doing some kind of healing, I find that I'm doing some kind of slipping into negative thinking and feelings. Fortunately, I have the tools to deal with those feelings now. I don't shut them off when I feel uncomfortable about a situation. I don't drink away my emotions. I face them and I deal with them.

For me it's important to remember that you never get cured. You can always heal and stay in a healing frame. The first step for me is not to drink and do drugs: One day at a time. I can't see doing it any other way because for me the thought of never drinking for the rest of my life was a concept I couldn't grasp. I don't even want to think about whether or not I can grasp it today. I don't have to. I just have to think about today. I have a real passion for living. It's real important for me to focus on today, and today I'm okay.

I think the biggest lesson for me is being real—I'm into being real right now. That involves experiencing pain, and I don't like it. Even if it's healthy, I don't like it. There was a time when I used to run from it. I just created another kind of pain from booze and drugs. The pain of unreality was killing me.

I can enjoy my emotions now, feel my fears and deal with them. I don't always want to do it, but I face it, I handle it and I take care of it as best I can. There are a lot of times I don't want to do the next right thing. I've learned that I don't need to like it to do it. My behavior is no longer the slave of my emotions. I still get urges to be self-destructive. Once in a while I'll give myself permission to eat too much ice cream and candy, or hit a movie and have too much buttered popcorn. I'm slowly upgrading my compulsions to be less harmful. I'm learning to take time out regularly and read a book, watch TV, or just be still and do nothing.

My eight years of sobriety have been a great adventure, much more powerful than any drink or drug. Being able to see and feel the beauty and joys of life help me to deal with the fears and pain that are also a part of my life. I know now I am always responsible for my behavior. I'm able to be a good friend to others and myself thanks to the love and respect for life sobriety has given me.

Chapter VI

RELAPSE

I've been taking off and landing
But this airport's closed
And how much thicker this fog is
   gonna get
God only knows
Just when you think that you've got a grip
Reality sneaks off, it gives you the slip

—John Hiatt
"Buffalo River Home"

When I first admitted I was an alcoholic, I thought the worst was over. Painfully, however, I realized the true misfortune was yet to come.

It was hard to admit that I had a drinking problem. After all, I drank the same as my friends. They were doing just fine. I was the only one screwing up. *It must be something else,* I thought. Truth is, most of my friends had a drinking problem, too, no matter how successful they were.

I went through the meetings and came to the stark realization that I was an alcoholic. I often heard the 12 Steps recited at the openings of meetings I attended, about two a week. That was the extent of my recovery program. I didn't have a sponsor in the beginning. I didn't read the big book. I did a half-assed job of it.

It has been said before in these pages that we slip when we aren't working the Steps and we don't have the faith that God can restore us to sanity. A couple of words that I disliked when I first hit meetings were *alcoholic* and *God*. I have since grown to embrace the meanings of each, but during the infancy of my recovery, I was scared to death of them.

When I entered recovery, I was ignorant of the process. It's a process of becoming well again. I didn't realize that. I thought I'd be fine if I just stopped drinking. I didn't need to work on anything else. Drinking was the root of my problems. I admitted that. I thought I just needed to find the way to get rid of this obsession and I'd be fine.

Steven Tyler mentioned how he felt when he was trying to cop his drugs. I remember when a friend would tell me he knew someone who had a great bag of pot. He'd call me during the afternoon or talk to me the night before, and we would try to track down this golden ounce. We would exhaust ourselves trying to find this catch, driving an hour with impaired vision or waiting home all night for a phone call. If we scored the bag at the very end of the night, after spending the whole day tracking it down, our day was complete. I spent all of my time and most of my thinking on that course.

Yet I would spend less than an hour in a meeting, twice a week, learning about a disease that had complete control of me. Two hours. That's it. No wonder I kept slipping.

As corny as it sounds, and as much as I never wanted to hear it when I was first in recovery, if you follow the 12 Steps and employ the inventories, and if you get a sponsor who works with you, not only are you bound to beat the obsession to drink, but you will improve every facet of your life. I guarantee it.

The reason I kept slipping is because I didn't know how to work the program. I didn't get a sponsor at first; that was for the other people sitting at the table. They looked like they were in worse shape than I was anyway. They could get a sponsor and take inventories and get God into their lives. I didn't have time for that.

The truth is at first I was afraid to ask someone to be my sponsor. I was afraid they would say no. Even though I displayed a hard shell on the outside, I was a fragile person on the inside. I was desperately crying out for help. It's just that my shell wouldn't let my true feelings emerge.

I never realized all the fear that filled my mind. Drinking was a way to stifle the fear, to shut it down. When I drank, I didn't have to think of reality; I could live in my fantasy world. But when I became sober—BOOM—reality hit me in the face. Had I followed the steps and run a rigid program from the get-go, I most likely would have taken hold of the magic and would have been fine. But fear captured my attention. I had this insatiable urge to drink. My mind was driving me crazy. Larry Gatlin mentioned it earlier: my disease was beginning to talk to me. It convinced me that I could have a couple drinks and I'd be all right. I didn't have to get drunk, it said, just a couple of cold ones.

I was paranoid about going into a bar. Everyone knew I was sober. My friends, coworkers, people at meetings—they all thought I was sober. I was the only one holding onto the dark news. I couldn't go to a bar or a club and enjoy myself for a while and drink. I'd keep looking around hoping I wouldn't be recognized. I couldn't go home and drink. My wife wouldn't allow it. The only place I could drink was the car. How's that for a suicide mission? The only place I could get messed up was behind the wheel. The thought of getting pulled over for drunk driving, or the notion that I might hurt someone, took a back seat to my disease. My mind was plotting the mission. I couldn't drive around with a beer bottle in my hand, or a wine cooler. I wasn't crazy about either one of those. My drink of choice was vodka. I wanted the liquor.

So I bought two large iced teas, poured half of them out in the parking lot of the party store and replaced the harmless beverage with booze. As I drove, it looked as though I was taking a cold refreshing plunge with Nestea. Actually, I was going out of my mind. I'd drink two of those in 10 or 15 minutes and I'd get hit pretty good. Then I'd work on the breath mints.

Remember, paranoia was pretty high at this point. I had to concentrate on the laws of the road—speed limit, stopping at red lights, not crossing the yellow line—everything we learn in school, plus hiding the rancid vodka breath; that was very important. I could never smell of alcohol or it would be all over. So I loaded myself with breath mints. I'd pop handfuls of Tic Tacs until two boxes were gone, then I'd pop the Certs. I'd carry a tube of toothpaste in the car, too.

It didn't take long for my wife to catch on. She made me call my sponsor and tell him the truth. He was very forgiving and talked me through my guilt and shame. I felt good after we talked.

He really cared for my well-being. But within a couple days I was doing it again. After getting caught a couple more times, I knew the gig was up. My life was absolutely miserable. I was close to a divorce, my wife and daughter were going to leave, my sponsor fired me. He warned me. He said if I kept slipping, there wasn't anything he could do for me. I was all alone. I really didn't want to drink anymore.

The next day I was on my way home from work. I passed the usual party store where I bought the booze. I didn't turn in that day. I felt good about that. But it's amazing how this disease works when it calls you. I was amazed at how many liquor stores popped up on the way home. There must have been a couple dozen of them. I was fighting this all the way home. Talk about a monkey on my back. I thought

King Kong was reaching his arm out from every liquor store, trying to drag me in. I prayed to get home. Just straight from work to the apartment. That's all I wanted.

I wound up in the parking lot of the party store. I really didn't want to drink. I didn't want to screw up my life anymore. It wasn't fun anymore. The thrill was gone. But my disease was calling me. I closed my eyes and began to pray. Not the surface prayers that I had been accustomed to in the past: I really prayed. I closed my eyes tight, clasped my hands together and concentrated. I really prayed hard, asking God to remove the desire to drink. Remove it right then and get me home safe and sober. I meant it with all my heart and soul. It was the deepest prayer of my life.

Immediately I felt this sense of relief overtake my body. I started to tingle from my feet to my eyebrows. The obsession was lifted immediately. That was my first true miracle of sobriety. I haven't had a drink since.

I severed ties with everyone I'd been drinking with. It was one of the best things I ever did. Good friends are a lot like tennis: if you play tennis with a better player, you become better. My drinking buddies had no ambitions or career goals. They had great pot, though, and they were funny. We had a lot of laughs. But they didn't care about me or my feelings. I really didn't care about theirs, either.

I now hang out with people I truly admire, who live a terrific program I can learn from, who are constant examples of what I want to be. Just like the tennis player, my game is improving every day.

I've known Eddie Money since his first tour with the J. Geils Band in 1978. We've spent the last few years talking about sobriety and our kids, a big change from our past. Eddie had always been one of rock 'n' roll's most lively subjects to interview. On this occasion, I spent the day in his California home playing with the kids, driving in his car listening to his new demo tapes, and sitting on his patio doing this interview.

It took Eddie several relapses to get straight. We often shared our experiences with each other. He would call and ask, "You still slipping and sliding?" Then he'd tell me he was taking it a day at a time, that he was a "Clean Machine." I selected this interview because of his rigorous honesty. He was real proud of achieving a year of sobriety. A big hurdle. As you'll soon discover, this is Eddie at his best.

Earnie Larsen is the pioneer of Stage II Recovery, a phenomenal addition to the original 12-Step recovery program, or Stage I as Earnie refers to it. I must admit Stage II requires a lot of work, but as Earnie puts it, "Michael Jordan practiced and practiced to be a great ball player. Why would anyone spend a few minutes a day on their recovery program, which really is their practice program?"

His Stage II work has had monumental success in recovery programs, opening the inner problems that cause us to drink and use in the first place. He asks a lot of very important questions. It's up to us to answer them honestly and continue practicing on the results.

Eddie Money

Eddie Money is a recovering alcoholic and drug addict. He's been selling millions of records and performing sold-out concerts around the world since 1977.

Right now I have a year.
I have a year because I don't hang
around with people who get high.
I don't have any booze in the icebox.
I'm not around the same people
I used to hang with.

By the grace of God I have a year. I'll tell you, I've been nine months three times. I'd go out on the road, find a little chickie, someone would offer me some toot and that was the end of that.

First time I had seven months. I got out of rehab back in 1987. Funny part about it was when "Take Me Home Tonight" came out on the radio, I was doing dishes in a rehab, setting tables, and I said, "What's wrong with this picture?" When I got out of there, it was wonderful to be straight. It was very hard at first. It was hard not being able to smoke pot or do toot or drink because I was a musician and that's what we used to do.

Then I had seven months, and I slipped when I had a really bad bronchial attack. I had bronchial asthma and I did some cough medicine because I was sick. The next day, I wanted to get some more, so I found the doctor who was on the road—Dr. Feelgood. I think it was in Cincinnati and I got some Tuscadan, which is like heroin in a teaspoon. I mean, this stuff makes you nod and scratch; it's just like junk. I did some of that and I did a three-hour show. Then, after that, the guy who was taking me to the hospital to get my chest x-rayed was the runner for the gig, the blow dealer for the gig. That's when I fell off the wagon.

Then I got straight again and stayed straight for about nine months. I met a girl on the road and she was really super straight. I love sex on cocaine and we stayed straight for about four or five days and I said, "Hey, have you ever tried it on blow?" This chick was hot. So I copped some blow and I was on a run for a week. She thought I was completely out of my mind and she left me.

Then I stayed straight for another nine months and took it really seriously. I left my previous wife and fell in love with Laurie, my present wife. I met her in Nashville. I liked Laurie because she was very straight. When I did cocaine she didn't know what it was. She didn't drink, she didn't smoke, and she's got a great little body on her. At that point, I was so high I was straight. I used to drink to bring my nervousness down from the blow, then I'd smoke pot to maintain a certain level. I wasn't really getting high anymore. I was getting the first buzz, but I wasn't incoherent. It's not like I couldn't work. I never drank when I went on stage. I always had somebody on the side of the stage with some toot for me in the middle of the set. I used the reward syndrome. I worked straight, then after work I'd get out of my fucking mind.

I had left my wife and I fell in love with Laurie, who was seven months pregnant. I wanted to have a baby. I wanted to get my life back together. At the same time I was getting ready to make the album *Nothing to Lose,* and I couldn't make another record stoned because the record company was really getting pissed off. The management company was getting really adamant about me getting too high and too crazy, so I started going to meetings again. I was going to meetings and maintaining. I wasn't doing any toot.

I used to be into a lot of pornography. I used to love porno—you know, imagination. Pornography is a spiritual slip, that's what it is.

When you watch porno movies, it's the same thing as if you're doing blow and drinking or smoking pot because of the high you get off of your imagination running as wild as it does. It'll eventually lead you back to getting high again. That's exactly what happens.

So I cut most of that out, but Laurie went into false labor and I was stoned on pot. I was staying away from everything else. I was staying away from coke, but I was stoned on some pot when she went into false labor. I was high and it freaked me out so much that I decided to really take my life seriously. I managed to stay straight for nine more months.

At one point, I was up to seven grams a day, snorting; never free-based in my life. I was snorting seven grams of blow a day. I was smoking a lot of weed and drinking about two six-packs of beer a day, and maybe a fifth of vodka every two days, Stoli on the rocks.

I would stay up all night on toot and wait for the liquor store to open at six. I drank until my dealers got up at nine-thirty, ten. If I ran out of one dealer I went to the next. I was just a total wreck, a total wreck.

I'd get home after a tour and run into my old connections. I was doing some heavy drinking in a bar and smoking Persian—Pers, they call it. It's a liquid heroin that you put on tin foil. You light a match under it and it runs down the tin foil, then you smoke it up in a tin foil pipe you roll up. It's called chasing the dragon and I was doing a lot of that. When that wasn't around I started snorting some heroin.

One night I was really drunk and I went to a club in Oakland and snorted some Penatol, which is like a bathtub barbiturate. It didn't mix with the alcohol I had in me. I went into a semi-coma. I fell asleep with my leg in an awkward position and when you're that stoned, your nerves don't twitch. I killed the sciatic nerve in my left leg and knocked my kidneys out. A lot of doctors told me I was never going to walk again.

But by the grace of God, my perseverance and a lot of physical therapy, I came back. I ran into a doctor in San Francisco who took care of my leg and he said, "You'll be walking again. A year from now you'll be hopping around the streets, you'll be copping again." I thought he was crazy. I thought he was out of his mind. I never was going to get high again. Sure enough, a year later I was out on the streets getting loaded again—with a cane.

I was in a rock band when I was young and I never got high. When I got out of high school, I went into the police department as a police trainee. That's when I first started getting loaded. My father was Patrolman of the Year. I was getting high when I was in the police department. I was smoking a lot of pot. I wrote this letter to my friends on carbon paper. Some people in the police department read the carbon paper—there was a lot of stuff mentioning drugs in there. It was quite an embarrassment for my father. I got scared and quit the police department. I moved out to California and kind of straightened up and maintained.

When I was a kid I was always into rock 'n' roll. I wanted to be famous. I always thought that I had a good voice. I was a great harmonica player and I thought I was a pretty decent songwriter, and that came first. The drugs weren't in the picture.

I never really snorted cocaine until I had the money, until maybe my second record, *Life for the Taking*. Even then, I never did cocaine because I thought it was a waste of money. But then slowly, into *Playing for Keeps,* I developed a really bad habit of snorting coke. And you know, I have to say, I love the high cocaine gives me, I love the feeling that marijuana gives me and I love the buzz from a couple of beers, but I don't want to give up what I have now. I have serenity and my sobriety. This is something new for me, like when getting high was all new and great. It was wonderful. It's easy to slip. This recovery thing is a full-time gig, and a lot of people don't want to put themselves into that.

Right now I have a year. I have a year because I don't hang around with people who get high. I don't have any booze in the icebox. I'm not around the same people I used to hang with. I'm around Laurie. I'm around my kids. I hang around people from meetings. By the grace of God, next year I'll be straight; but I've got to take this one day at a time. This book might come out and, God forbid, I could be high. I hope not. I have to take it one day at a time.

When I go back out on the road is when it's going to be scary for me. That's when I'm going to have to be sure I hit a lot of meetings. I'm kind of glad everyone knows I'm straight because then I can't fuck up.

I think a rock star has to set an example for young people. I mean, the Beatles said it was okay to get stoned. Make love, not war. Tune in, turn on, drop out and all of that. That's what I grew up with. We lost a lot of people—Jim Morrison, Janis Joplin, Pig Pen from the Grateful Dead. You never think it can happen to you.

I'm still on shaky ground. I'm not on shaky ground today, and I wasn't on shaky ground last week. I don't think I'll be on shaky ground tomorrow. But two months down the road, I might be on shaky ground. I am not that well. I know I'm not going to get high today. I know I'm probably not going to get high next week or the week after.

I worry about getting loaded when I'm out on the road. But this time I'm a lot stronger. Having a year under my belt is quite an accomplishment. I don't want to give up that one year. I don't want to give up what I have. I don't want to start over. This is the new me. I'm proud of the fact that I can sustain this. I feel like an adult. I'm a man. I'm not a kid anymore. I gave up all those things that I used to lustfully enjoy. Now I feel like I've matured. I hope it's all part of my past.

It's great having these kids. It's time I grew up and settled down. I don't think that I really have changed that much. The only thing that has changed about me is that I don't use chemicals. I don't drink and I don't use drugs.

Thank God my outlook on life hasn't changed that much. I still look in the rearview mirror and try to do 95 and get away with it.

Earnie Larsen

Earnie Larsen has been intimately involved with people in 12-Step programs for over 30 years. He continues to trek across the country, conducting his mind-opening seminars. He's the author of over 30 books, including the breakthrough discovery *Stage II Recovery*, a must-read book that searches beyond the foundation of the 12 Steps and enhances personal recovery.

If you translate "program"
it means "practice." There's nothing
mystical about program. All program
means is practice. Then you think,
What are the criteria for an effective
practice program? *It could be your kids*
learning to shoot hockey pucks or
learning the computer. I came up
with four criteria that make
sense to me.

119

knew, as it says in the Big Book, I was at a point where I needed to do further work with these underlying habits and patterns. If I didn't, I would either relapse or switch addictions. I just couldn't find the serenity. I didn't know how to do that. I found that nobody else did, either. I asked everyone I knew, "How do you do this?" because after 12 years of working a hard program I wound up in a psych unit. I had absolutely no idea what in the world got me there. I was going to meetings, I was reading the Big Book, I was talking to my sponsor, I had done several Fourth and Fifth Steps, I had heard thousands of fifth steps . . . but something was unhealed. I had no idea what it was and, therefore, I had absolutely no idea what to do about it.

I was being a priest with about four full-time jobs. I was certainly one of the best-known religious writers in the country, selling millions of books and traveling the country, practicing my addiction in the name of God and spirituality, and had absolutely no idea what was going on.

I went to all the old-timers I knew and asked them, "All right, what would you do, what would you tell somebody?" They've been sober for two years, six years, ten years, 30 years, and they say, "I finally understand that I have a lot of anger," or "I have a lot of perfection-ism," or "I have a lot of workaholism" or "I cannot touch with my feel-ings." What do they tell people to do? The only answer I've ever found is, "More meetings, keep it simple, read the Big Book, talk to your sponsor." Well, if you tell a workaholic perfectionist to work harder, you're not going to get anywhere.

When I talk about this work, when it's specifically related to the 12 Steps, this is a deepening of Steps Six and Seven. I call them the for-gotten steps. When you talk about your character defects, Step Six, what are they? What's their nature? In the Fourth and Fifth Step, it doesn't say what crimes you've committed. It says you've shared the exact nature of your problems. What is the nature? I think the nature is always about the real underlying habits and patterns that truly have become habits, habits we've subconsciously learned in a very intense training program—the family of origin that has left deep, deep affec-tive scars, emotional scars that can only be dealt with by doing what is called inner child work. If you don't do that kind of work, which is what we call the technology of Stage II, you never close the circles.

There are a lot of people who lose their desire to drink and still have very unsatisfying lives in the sense that they can't carry on relationships, have terrible difficulty with intimacy, or become huge egomaniacs. Basically they just wind up switching their addiction. They become addicted to work, they become addicted to the program, they become addicted to all kinds of stuff.

The serenity, the real depth, is not there if you don't do the kind of work that uncovers what is causing the pain. So the criterion is not simply that I do or do not have a desire to drink. Some people never lose the desire to drink—that's biochemical, but that's not the criterion. I think the criterion has much more to do with real deep serenity or real deep spirituality, learning to truly care and love yourself so that you can truly reach out to other people. It's not limiting the 12 Steps; it's a different technology.

Step One of the 12 Steps is about pain. And I truly, truly did not want to go back to lockup. That's what motivated me. I didn't want to go back and be locked up in the psych unit. I also didn't want to keep having the migraine headaches and the bleeding ulcers and the feeling that every day was such a doggone struggle that I didn't know how I was going to get through it. But I'll be damned if I knew what to do about it. Clichés like "turn it over" (being a cliché doesn't mean it's not true) are the most wonderful advice in the world. I just didn't know how to turn it over. It says to turn your life over to the care— not to the power, not to the wisdom—of God as you understand him. Well that presupposes you have a capacity to accept that somebody could care about you. I didn't have that. Nobody had taught me that.

The life I was living was absolutely alone. I was out there by myself; there really wasn't any community. I was being transferred every year to plug a hole. I don't think they still teach that, but back in the 1960s they did. Holiness was separation from people. You didn't need family, you didn't need relationships; all you needed was to love God.

I've found in the 30 years of doing this work, of really trying to get people to go to some depth, that most people's concept of God is simply their dad with a God mask. No matter what they think God is, they still won't turn their life over, they're still praying for gifts. If you really believe that God is all loving, you don't pray for gifts; the gift is already given. What you pray for is your increased ability to accept the gift that is already there.

What you find when you work with people to try to get some depth is that by and large, unless they've really done some good work, God is their dad with a God mask. Until you take that God-mask off, and really look at what is behind it and do some changing, God as any kind of a personal, loving God just isn't there. So what you get is fear, guilt, worry and shame. If you relapse, you get terrible fear that God's going to turn his or her back on you. But see, that's not God; that's what happened to you when you learned authority does that as a father figure. But it isn't God. If your perception is toxic and your belief is toxic, then the consequence is going to be toxic. Then you have a toxic God.

So I started looking. I really started digging. I went to all the wise people that I could and asked and talked, and I really started listening to me, to what my heart was telling me. At that time there was a program around called Marriage Encounter. It's a religious program that had a lot to do with dialogue.

But again, it's Stage I. It's used in a slip or it's used when you feel you're going to have a slip. I found what I really needed was a much more ongoing relationship with a real sponsor or dialogue partner who was not dealing with crisis situations, but really trying to get to know me. People were starting to talk about family of origin. It's one of the most commonsense principles in the world—what you rub up against rubs off on you. That isn't exactly nuclear science. People started looking at family systems and where you come from. We did a little bit of that in the psych unit. It was interesting to me that first night in group. I was so ashamed about being there. Here I was, a priest with degrees, writing books and running around, and I'm locked up with these loonies. I say that affectionately, you know, because I was locked right up there with them. The guy next to me said, "What's your life like?" and I said, "Normal," and everybody laughed. I never got over how hilarious that is, being laughed at by guys in a locked psych unit.

Then he said, "Tell me about normal. Normal isn't healthy, normal's just what you do so often it's the norm." In my case, I had four full-time jobs; it was nuts! No wonder I had migraine headaches and bleeding ulcers. But then the really important question under that is, "Why are you doing this?"

It seems to me that spiritual power only comes from people who are truly at peace with themselves. This is a program of attraction, not promotion. Maybe I suppose everybody's blessed with different gifts. Maybe there are people who don't have to do this work. It just may happen. But in order for me to come to peace with myself and to learn to accept me and love me, I have to know me. I really have to know me. I never knew where the broken part was. I never knew where the toxic beliefs were. I never knew where the inner children were lost. I just didn't know. And so, all of those years in seminary and the priesthood, I was abusing the most tender part of me. It damn near died. In the name of holiness, in the name of spirituality, I didn't know me. I never, never knew how to come to know *me*.

I have come to really understand that I was never allowed to believe the importance of compassion as a little child. I had wonderful parents. I loved my family, but it was a Depression family. It was hard times. And you had to be tough. The dark side of that—because it isn't all bad, of course—is you move out of your body. It's too painful living in your body and being tough all the time and never allowing yourself to cry, never allowing pain to stop you. You stand there, by God, and you never give in. If your body is too painful to live in, you're going to leave.

So you go to your head or you go somewhere else, but you disconnect from your body. Well, how can you have compassion and how can you treat yourself well if you're not in your body? I have come to learn that there are major portions of me that I really need to learn to re-parent and to treat well, to be kind to me. I don't always have to do the hardest thing to prove that I can do it. I really believe that God is a loving God, that God doesn't love me more if I'm writing ten books a year as opposed to writing no books. God loves me. But that is a major shift in self-perception. Coming to grips with those wounded parts is tough. There's the image of a little child out there, buried under a mountain of petrified tears. Fifty years old. And I have to find that child. I have to nurture that child. I have to get that child to where he can trust me because *I'm* the one who's been abusing him for the last 30 years without realizing it. God must be sitting up there crying his eyes out. *You're beating the hell out of that kid in my name? Holy cow, read Scripture. When did I ever beat up a little kid?* But it was the best I had. I didn't know any better.

When I talk to recovery groups, there's this tremendous gratitude, and yet, if you ask by a show of hands, "How many of you feel like you still have a hole in your heart?" damn near all of them put their hands up. I ask them to list 15 or 20 typical issues that they have in there and to rate themselves on a score of one to ten; ten is high. Things like control, fear, repressed anger, difficulty with relations, fear of intimacy, workaholism, perfectionism, fear of abandonment, always feeling that sense of alienation and body shame: all that kind of stuff. I go through about half a dozen of them and stop to ask if anyone has a five on any of these and everyone says, "Oh my God, I've got 15 on all of them." And I say, "Doesn't it hurt?" They nod their heads. All these issues are obstacles to spirituality.

It's difficult talking to people about the pain they feel. We think life's supposed to hurt, which is true for a lot of us. That says a lot about spirituality and how much you really believe in the power of an all-loving God. We think we're supposed to hurt like this. We just really don't know what to do about it. We don't even know how to talk about it.

"What comes from the heart touches the heart." Beautiful old program saying. When you start talking to people and say, "Touch your own heart. Do you have these issues? Do they cause you pain? Does it ever give you a lot of hurt thinking that you are passing these same traits onto your kids and that they'll pass them on to their kids? Then why are those traits there? You've been working your programs for 8 years, 10 years, 12 years, 20 years—why are they still there?" And of course there's not much of an answer to that.

That speaks to me. Whether it's sex or work or the egomaniac business, that speaks to me again of hurts not healed, and not nearly so much as people being evil or anything. What that says to me is that there is a gaping hole down there that's not being healed; it's ulcerating out in our lived life. And therefore, again, what that says to me is, how do we get back to that wound? What is the wound? There's something there that isn't healed and it's blocking my serenity.

I think a truly spiritual person is a healed person. That person has found peace and serenity. It just kind of makes sense that if you've got a wound in you that's oozing pus, you're not going to be at peace. I've really been trying to work on and figure that out. I've been sharing with my group, and a lot of guys are doing this work—how do you get back and find out what is really wounded so you can heal it? What is that? You can call it Step Four. You can call it Step Six. It's certainly not anti-12 Step, but it's a depth that ordinarily you're never going to get to in the 12 Steps.

Even if you can't share everything verbally, if you write something, or record it and just play it back to yourself, just verbalizing out loud what you have written is ten times more powerful than just writing it.

Writing it is ten times more powerful than just thinking it. And even more so if you can take that tape and share it with a trusted other person. That gets you feedback and it's ten times more powerful.

There's a lot of toxic love out there because there's a lot of fear. There's a lot of anger and there's a lot of shame. That's what creates toxic relationships. I think the reason is that it defines who we are. Who we choose in relationships is much more about who *we* are than who *they* are.

Shame and all those related terms mean we have internalized a belief that we really don't deserve to be loved and can never really be loved. People think they're kind of dumb, so somebody intelligent never would really love them. Or the millions upon millions of people who learn that close is not safe: How can I outperform that? Who does that leave me to be in a relationship with? If I don't deserve to be loved and have somebody present to me, then the only person I can choose to be with is somebody who will not be emotionally present to me. I don't have a choice about anything else. God knows, there are a million of these people out there. I think that's just a real fundamental principle: relationships and who we choose are much more about us than it is about them.

We tend to become one parent and marry the other. A lot of times the boy will become the father and marry a woman who becomes the mother, or vice versa with the daughters. I don't think it necessarily goes that boys marry their mother, but they do become one parent and marry the other.

You know the old program saying, and by God it's absolutely true, "You don't have to know why you drink to stop." You've probably heard that a billion times and it's absolutely right. You sit there in your cups endlessly philosophizing about why you drink. You drink because you're an alcoholic. All you need to know is you have to stop. That's all you need to know for sobriety. If you're going to continue past that, however, you do need to know the origin, you need to know the various character defects that are going to cause a relapse or switched addiction or minimized serenity. But you don't need to know anymore to stop. Stage I is about Stage I. It's about stopping. It's about arresting an addiction. And you don't have to do family of origin stuff to stop drinking. You don't have to do inner child work to achieve sobriety. There are lots of people in program who are sober and haven't done any of that kind of work. If you're going to continue and really deepen your spirituality, then I think that other work needs to be done.

It's all evolution. I mean the 12 Steps are only 55 years old. Everything is evolution. I think 50 years down the road, some additional version is going to be every bit as much a part of program as Stage I is part of it now.

Chemicals medicate pain. When you get into addiction, it's not about curiosity. It's not about fun. It's about escaping pain. If a program only focuses on the medication, which is alcoholism, then what you have is a lot of pain. An analogy we used all the time at one of the hospital-based treatment centers I worked at was this: On the fourth floor they had a cancer unit and some poor guy's up there in terrible pain from bone cancer. He has a lot of morphine or other painkillers. Take his painkiller away and what's he got? Take the alcohol away from the alcoholic, what's he got? Sooner or later, your program needs to focus on pain—meaning low self-esteem, meaning self-hatred, meaning guilt, meaning shame, meaning grief, meaning all that kind of stuff—or you're going to go back to your pain reliever.

If you translate "program" it means "practice." There's nothing mystical about program. All program means is practice. Then you think, *What are the criteria for an effective practice program?* It could be your kids learning to shoot hockey pucks or learning the computer.

I came up with four criteria that make sense to me.

One is understanding. You're not going to get good at anything you don't understand. And what I'm talking about there, again in Stage II, is how well do you understand yourself? *How well do you understand your belief systems? How well do you understand where they came from? How well do you really know your own story?* And I find, doing lots of this kind of stuff around the country—take what you like and leave the rest—that most people fall off the wagon right there. They really don't understand. They don't understand where they are, they don't understand who they are, and therefore they don't understand what they need to do to change themselves.

The second criterion for any effective practice program is focus. A program that is not focused is not a program. What I'm talking about here are two things. First of all, what is the issue you're working on? If that's not specific, then you're not working on an issue. What I do in my seminars is say, "You have one second. I want you to turn to the person next to you and, in one second, tell that person the issue you've determined you're working on today. Okay, go." And of course, if you don't know, a second is not anywhere near long enough. If you do know, a second is plenty long. If you don't have an issue, you don't have a program.

In Stage I, you have an issue—stop drinking or stop coke or stop gambling, whatever the hell it is. That's why you make some progress; there's a focus. What if my focus is that I have a terrible time being honest about my feelings toward women? If that's the issue, what's the only way I'm going to get good at that? Again, this is not nuclear science. The only way you're going to get good at being honest with women is to practice every day at being honest with women. That's the difference between change behavior and support behavior; they aren't the same thing. Going to groups, spiritual reading—all that kind of stuff, by and large, is support behavior. But change behavior is behavior that you're doing that has the specific focus of learning a new skill. That's something very different. You can go to a group forever and talk good stuff and never make any progress.

The third criterion is consistency and practice. You cannot be consistent if you don't have a focus because what are you going to be consistent about without a focus?

The fourth criterion is accountability. If you don't have accountability and support, you're never going to be consistent about these specific behaviors. You really need some understanding that what you're doing is changing your basic perception about life.

None of this is as complicated as you may think. How did Michael Jordan get into basketball? How does anybody get good at anything? They practice. Why would your program be any different?

Chapter VII

DEPARTMENT OF YOUTH

This is no social crisis,
just another tricky day for you.

—Pete Townshend
"Another Tricky Day"

What Would You Say to High School Students?

*O*ur addictive personalities creep up on us early. Certain behaviors frequently arise in high school or middle school. Statistics suggest that more than eight million teenagers are alcoholics. Statistically, for them, it's normal to get drunk on weekends; it's acceptable to party and get blitzed at football games. In fact, for many it's expected. Then they drive home with a loaded blood-alcohol level. Just another Friday night.

I was the same way. The prevalent groups in my high school were the jocks and the burnouts. I never tried out for the football team, nor was I the typical burnout. I became a loner. I didn't hang around the jocks because they didn't smoke pot. I couldn't put up with the burnouts. Couldn't they at least wash their hair? But I was ingesting just as much alcohol and as many drugs as they were.

My daily ritual was to get to school at 7:30 in the morning, go to the smoking lounge and pass around a few joints. Then I went to my first-hour trigonometry class. No wonder I failed math.

I didn't see the pattern of addiction settling in. If my drug and alcohol use was the dominant pattern, the underlying feelings of fear and inadequacy were sizzling under the surface. I didn't know that. I do know that once I became educated about the diseases of alcoholism and drug addiction, my using was never the same. Education took away the splendor, the freedom. Responsibility set in—the same responsibility that I often shielded behind the mask of addiction.

I thought my behavior was normal in high school because my friends were doing the same thing. I remember hearing the principal on the Monday morning announcements telling us that one of my friends was found dead in a swamp behind the school after a football game. He passed out and drowned in a few inches of water. That doesn't happen when you're sober.

I continue to see more and more high school kids attending recovery meetings and supporting each other with their programs. They have a head start on many of us. I've often wished I had done something about it when I was much younger.

But that's okay for me. I'm grateful that I discovered sobriety when I did. The timing was perfect. I had to go through what I went through to fully appreciate the value of a recovery program. Now I cherish it.

When I was in high school, I seemed to be out of touch with many things. I led my life with blinders on. I was arrogant and self-centered, caring about nothing except how things would affect me. Perhaps had someone I admired pulled me aside and let me know what was going on, I might have listened. It could have changed my life.

I asked many of the people in the book if they would pass on some advice and wisdom to young people. Specifically, what would they say to a group of high school kids about alcoholism and addiction?

Doug Fieger

What would I tell a gathering of high school students? I'd tell them you have to do what you have to do. I hope you don't do what I did. I'd tell them that I grew up in a family that was very violent. I grew up scared. I grew up feeling different. I grew up feeling that I had a hole in my gut. I found that if I got high, that hole shrunk.

At first, getting high was exciting and fun. Then it became my job. It became the thing that I did for a living, every day—actually for dying. That's what I did—I died a little bit, but I couldn't die.

Because I couldn't die something had to give. It eventually drove me to madness, to serious and true madness. And I can't believe that I'm psychotic at all. I believe that I'm a very considered person intellectually. I think that I have ability, that I was given a mind and I've educated it. I believe that I have a spirit that isn't twisted. I believe that my spirit is whole and beautiful. Yet running from how I felt caused me to damage my intellect and my soul—my spirit. I found out that there was a way in which I didn't have to do that anymore.

It's my profound wish that if these kids are anything like me, they will find that way as well. There are those of us who can tell them what we did.

Ritch Shydner

For a long time I never knew there was another way to go. I never knew it. I was in pain. If somebody had said, "If you think you have a problem with alcohol or drugs, you do," I might have asked for help because I knew that I had a problem when I was 16. If anyone had said, "You can come talk to these people and they understand about it because they've been through it"—not like somebody who's going to look down at you and say you've got a problem, that you're weak, you're stupid—I might have gone.

If you're sick of it and it doesn't take away the pain that it first took away—if you've got to think about that—then you've got a problem. I wish there was somebody standing there for me who said they were lucky enough to live through it.

Mike Binder

I would tell them to look in the mirror in the morning and learn to tell yourself you love yourself. Take the time every day and just put your arms around yourself, give yourself a hug, or look in the mirror and throw yourself a kiss. Self-hate is the biggest problem with kids. It was my biggest as a kid.

I would tell them to love yourself, to treat yourself really good and to just say, "Bill or Kay, you know, I love you, you're a good person," and scruff up your own head. I remember when my sponsor told me to do that in the mirror and one morning I gave myself the finger.

I couldn't even blow myself a kiss.

Learn to love yourself. Really learn to trust the potential you have as a human being, and make your goal being the best person you can be. We're all God's projects. God has so many projects going. He's the busiest guy in the world. Each one of us is a project. Our goal should be to make that project the best project that God can have. Not the best project of all his projects, but the best that project can be. That's all we are.

We're here to experience something for him, for the universe. The goal should be to be the best you can be. Nothing more. It's not to be better than the guy down the street, or be the most famous or the richest; just be the best you can be.

One of the reasons we're so unhappy when we're doing drugs and alcohol is because in our heart we know we're not reaching our full potential. We know we're not doing God's will for him. You know it, you feel it, your body vibrates with it. So the goal is to do God's will, to be the best Mike or the best Dave or the best Karen you can be, so you can best serve God, so you can best implement God's plan for your life.

My biggest thing was accepting that I wasn't the greatest comedian in America. I wanted to be because I figured if I was, everyone would love me. I had to come to terms with the fact that I was who I was and got as far as I got and that God wasn't going to let me down. It was okay just being me. You know, Robin Williams was doing fine. So was Howie Mandell. I'm not going to compare myself to anybody. I had to accept who I am because that was my biggest problem: I wanted to be a famous comedian.

But that wouldn't have done it. If I'd become famous when I was 22, I'd be dead now. No doubt in my mind, I'd be dead. I wasn't ready to handle it. My biggest problem was accepting the fact that I was where I was supposed to be and no further. I wasn't supposed to be any further or any richer or any cooler.

Larry Gatlin

I did it. I can't help it. It's over. I had a lot of fun doing it, but it turned into a nightmare, into misery.

God helped me out of the pit. Some of you are going to listen, some of you are not. Some of you are going to try it anyway. Some of you are too smart to listen to me or anybody else and you're just going to try it on your own. If you have tried it and you've got a problem, there's a way out. And mainly, you can have a lot of fun and have a wonderful life without doing drugs. It's that simple.

Tony Sales

I guess I'd say to turn to your friend to the left or right and tell that person you care about them. Tell them that if they ever need you, you'll be there for them. And possibly, if they do likewise, if we all experience more helping each other out in the world, we won't have to turn to drugs and alcohol. You can make it. You can have a prosperous and happy life without the use of substance. Try it and see.

Tai Babilonia

Set a goal for yourself and try to achieve it the best that you can. Stick to it. I really think that keeps you out of trouble. Sports is a great idea. First of all, it's healthy and it's fun. The rewards are great if you just stick to it.

Eddie Money

The first thing I'd say to them is if you drink and you get caught drinking, you're going to lose your license. If you get high and you get caught getting high, you'll never work for Bell Telephone or IBM. This society will take away what you think you might want in the future. I would tell them the same thing a cop would tell them. I would have to say, "Hey, you can go out there and do all this shit, but if you get caught, you're fucked." That would make them think real quick.

I wouldn't tell them how great it is to be straight. I would tell them how horrible it is to be strung out and to drink so much that you don't get drunk. You smoke so much pot that you don't even get high on it; it just becomes a bad habit. That you'll need so much coke to get high on, it'll cost you a fortune. I won't tell them that because they won't listen to that. I'll just tell them, "Hey man, I got real fucking high and I almost could never walk again. I got so high that I almost went broke and my career was almost over. I learned my lesson the hard way, and I mean the hard way." I think they'd get hip to that.

Jack Scalia

Learn to believe in yourself. Find the people around you who are supportive. As human beings, we've all been given by God a thing called instinct. When I was a kid growing up and I was with my friends, someone would say—because I always had a very strong arm—"Jack, I bet you can't break that window." And you know, there was a little bell that always went off that said it was wrong, but I'd pick up the rock and then throw it most of the time.

So honor your instincts and just find people who are supportive of you. The ones who berate or neglect, or don't offer support or encouragement, avoid them.

Lou Gossett Jr.

I'd say more than just say no. I'd say if you need to get high because your best friend gets high, you're not in school doing what you should be doing. And that's searching for getting high on information and education that'll make you higher than you ever could imagine. If you're not happy inside, you have to do something about that, but there's nothing outside that's going to fix you; only you can fix that—from the inside.

Whatever you have to do to fix the inside, without putting anything outside in, that's what you have to do. You can't get there by altering your mind; you slip down the steps. So why don't you be the shining example for your best friend and say this is the way to go, this is the way to manhood or womanhood, not that way. That'll last maybe a couple minutes. This will last a lifetime.

Dallas Taylor

I'd open up introducing myself as an alcoholic and a drug addict because that's what I am. And I'd start out by saying that it's not my job to talk about the evils of drugs and alcohol and I'm not going to stand there and say you shouldn't do this or that.

What I have to say is simply what happened to me and what it was like for me to be a kid. Way before I took my first drink or smoked my first joint, I felt like the ugly duckling; I felt like the kid that didn't fit in. I was full of fear and self-loathing. I never felt a part of, never felt I belonged. And then I'd say that if you can identify with any of these feelings, then you may be like me.

Then I'd say I have close to six years sober, but I almost died as a result of my alcohol and drugs. That damage can be done far, far in advance of your realizing that you're past the point where it's too late. And that, yeah, living may not be something you want to do right now—in fact, most kids don't care about living; they're either immortal or they want to die. But there will be a point in your life when you might want to live. And you'll find out you can't, you're not going to because of the choices you made when you were young. I think that's how I would spend my first five minutes.

John Ratzenberger

Well, there's hope. Don't just give up because there are a lot of people in your situation. You're not the only one it's happening to. Find an organization that caters to people like you. There's no shame involved in it. You can go to meetings. There's no shame. No one's going to brand you a chicken or a tattletale or say, "Don't you have terrible parents?" because you do love your parents. Everybody loves their parents. Even children that are physically abused, you know, as unfortunate as it is, they love their parents. That's why people can take advantage of you. That's why they can call you stupid and you let them get away with it: because you love them. Because you love them get help for yourself. Then you'll be able to help them.

I remember hearing words of advice from successful people who were 43 years old when I was a kid and I never believed them. I said, "Ah, what's he know? He's got a lot of dough, he's 43 and over the hill." And I'm 20, 21 years old. I never listened to them, so I don't really suspect that kids out there today are going to listen to me either, but that's just the way it is.

John Hiatt

Listen to your own instincts. Listen to your own heart. To your own self be true. I had too many other voices going on in my head. Messages and crazy this and crazy that. I would say the best advice I could give a kid is to take care of yourself because you're worth it. You're definitely worth it.

Anthony Kiedis

The word partying is not necessarily synonymous with taking drugs and alcohol. It's become such a social synonym to say let's party, meaning let's get fucked up on drugs and alcohol, that it's kind of a concept that disturbs me. I didn't really start partying until I got clean. So I try to explain that having the good times and being with girls, or being out and dancing does not require, despite the myth, that you be inebriated or intoxicated on anything other than just life itself. Kids grow up in a society where it's just a given that if you want to have fun, if you want to have a good time, you get fucked up on drugs and alcohol. They don't even stop to think twice that they can have fun without them.

A big part of taking drugs and alcohol is doing something against your parents' will, which is a concept I believe in. I believe going against your parents is a natural part of growing up, and it's how you develop ideas of your own. It's healthy, but you don't have to do something to hurt yourself to show that you're different and that you don't have to be like them. That's self-defeating. Especially for kids who are into suicide. It's a picture-perfect example of, "Oh well, my Mom's an asshole (which she very well might be), so I'll slash my wrists and then she'll feel as bad as I feel." This is a concept that seems pretty standard among teenagers.

I'd talk about how wonderful life itself can be. You're sitting here, you have another warm person next to you that you can hug or that you could go do something with, and the importance of leaving yourself open to these experiences is immeasurable. Drugs and alcohol slowly but surely close that off.

Nils Lofgren

I'd just say to them that no matter what anyone thinks, it's really a fact that everybody at every age gets scared and fearful of who they are, what they are doing. It's all a learning process. It's okay to be who you are. You are enough, no matter what anyone tells you. You have to try to embrace that and go with whatever that is. If you're an outcast, just hang in there because there are people out there. Look for people who are like you or who can understand your feelings.

Look for people to talk to about what's bugging you. If you can't talk to your parents, find a friend. If all your friends think you're full of shit and they don't want to understand you and they don't think you have a valid point, find a friend that does. Find somebody to talk to, get it out. Go to a priest, go to a big brother, just find somebody to talk to because *you're enough*. That's my main thing today: *I'm enough*. No matter how little I do or how much I do, I'm okay. It's the hardest thing to feel when you're growing up. It's so sad because when they don't believe that "I'm enough," people go out and kill themselves. No matter how much pain you're in, you are enough just being who you are. If you can't get the love and respect you feel you need and you want from anybody in your life, get other people in your life. Take chances, open your mouth and, if the first 20 people dump on you, don't talk to them; find another 20 people. Keep taking chances until you find somebody you can talk to. That helps you realize you're not the only one with these feelings.

What it's all about—I remember growing up—is don't let them know how you really feel. I have to act this way or I won't fit in. I know about that need to want to fit in. There are no shortcuts, you have to go through that pain. Don't keep it to yourself. Don't think you're the only one who feels that way. If the only people in your life are making you feel bad and are humiliating you, get other people in your life. Don't hesitate to take whatever chances you have to because the consequences of not doing so are deadly, with and without drugs. Those crises exist.

I think the biggest thing is to find people to talk to, people who are going to look at you like they understand. Just being able to talk to somebody and get it out helps you to see it. You look at it in a way that you can't when you keep it all inside. Unfortunately, that's what most people do in high school, college or even if they are parents or grandparents: they keep so much inside.

Everything might look right on the outside, but it's all about how you feel inside. It wasn't until I got clean and sober that I was willing to face that question. I remember when they first started asking me how I felt. I didn't know.

Earnie Larsen

One of the sharpest swords you're ever going to have to deal with in your life is grief, which comes after having lost something that you're never going to get back. What a shame it is to waste your youth, to burn up those precious, precious years in all of the fear and the unconsciousness about chemical dependency. That induces all of the self-hatred, all of the lies and all of the lost opportunities. Whenever, if ever, you come out of this, you are going to look back with such grief—not guilt, necessarily, but such grief at having lost so many, many precious experiences and so many precious years out of your life. Of course, you won't know that until you're 30 or 40 or 50, looking back. It's planting time bombs out in front of you. You get there and they're going to blow up. You're planting them in your future.

Ozzy Osbourne

If you do stupid things, expect stupid results. I didn't think there was another life. I didn't honestly think that life was worth a shit without being fucked up. I couldn't accept the fact; I couldn't accept the world. I was living in fear. I was afraid of the world. People go, "Ozzy Osbourne—afraid? The wild man of rock 'n' roll?" But behind the fucking charade was a very scared person. What you have to do is to talk one-on-one with somebody else who's sober. You have to get rid of your fucking anxiety. You have to find someone to talk with.

Dennis Hopper

To me, using drugs and drinking is just a wasted life. If you use drugs and drink, life isn't really long enough to achieve a lot of things. You won't accomplish any of the things you want to accomplish. You might get there for some of the things, but you won't continue accomplishing them, and you'll spend your life wasting whatever creative time and family time you could have.

Getting alcohol and drugs is a major job. It's a full-time job. You don't get any rewards at the end of it because nobody will hire you. Nobody listens to you at a certain point.

Chris Mullin

I think kids are a little more educated about it because they're closer to it. They probably know someone who's involved in it. I'd tell them that it's okay, that they don't have to shoulder all the blame, that they're not alone. Kids feel isolated. To be able to deal with it, you have to be able to let it out. Getting help is okay. These days there are so many single-parent homes and a lot of obstacles. People need help just dealing with that. You don't have to shoulder this thing by yourself. Just get some help. I know it's a lot easier to say it, but if you just take that first step, you'll feel immediate relief.

Chapter VIII

BRING ON THE FAMILY

It's a sad man, my friend,
who's livin' in his own skin
and can't stand the company.

—Bruce Springsteen
"Better Days"

In many cases, the roots of our dysfunction often begin with our family history. When we grow up in a dysfunctional environment, we're bound to have a lot of problems unless we face our troubled upbringing and make changes to correct it.

Steven Tyler mentions something critical in "Final Thoughts" (chapter XI): we're all these computer disks and whatever our parents communicated to us—good, bad, positive or negative—we thought that was the correct way. It takes a long time to reprogram the disks.

China Kantner saw her mother at the end of both spectrums, from a raving rock 'n' roll lunatic to a straight-laced mom. The fact that her mother discovered a recovery program, China says, saved her own life from addiction. Mom herself, Grace Slick, says a few words of her own. John Ratzenberger ends this chapter with some brutal honesty about his childhood. John is one of only a few people in the book who is not a recovering alcoholic. He never had a drinking problem. His father's alcoholism, however, had a crucial impact on his upbringing and his adult life.

China Kantner

China Kantner is a recovering
alcoholic. She's a former MTV host
who is acting in numerous theatri-
cal releases. Her parents are musicians Grace Slick and Paul Kantner.

*I just came to my senses
and figured out that although I loved
alcohol more than anything in the
world, I should stop because I did
love it more than anything.*

I was with my girlfriend's boyfriend in his house. I
drank cooking sherry and got really drunk, threw
up all over the house. I called my mom and she came
and picked me up. I got in the car and said, "Mom, I
can't do this anymore, it's just ridiculous. I don't
know what I did with this guy. I don't know if I had
sex with him or what. I was in a blackout. I threw up
all over his house. I drank cooking sherry, which is
something nonalcoholics don't do. I think it's time I
go to a meeting."

I also think that a small part of me wanted to find
more friends. I wanted to find a place that felt like

home, which I really hadn't been feeling. It's not like I was this depressed kid, just confused. I had seen how meetings had made such a great example for friendships and for relationships, and I kind of wanted that. I'm not sure at that point if I really wanted to actually get sober. I wanted a circuit of close friends, so I went.

That was right before I spent my first summer in New York with MTV. I was staying with my mom's best friend, June. I didn't go to many meetings, but I was sober. At the end of the summer I met this guy. I was really excited because he was neat and I hadn't really had a boyfriend before. I was with this girl, who was my best friend at the time, and she really didn't understand alcoholics. We were at a dinner party one night and she said, "Have a glass of wine, it's not a problem." She was a big influence on me; I pretty much did whatever she told me because I looked up to her. So I said, "Sure, I guess I'll have one," and I felt kind of weird about it. I also felt kind of excited, like I was doing something bad. I knew I shouldn't be doing it but I did it anyway. Well, one ended up to be ten that night. I got drunk and went to a club with this guy and all his friends. June was taking care of me and I hadn't called her. It was about two in the morning by now. All of us were drunk.

I remember going to his hotel, and in between the club and the hotel I didn't remember anything. But then I remember looking up and seeing the elevator numbers when we were on our way up in the hotel. Then I blacked out again. I remember being in his hotel room with my two girlfriends and going to the bathroom and throwing up, having my friend hold my hair back and getting rug burns on my knees because I fell down. I couldn't walk. The next thing I remember is waking up in the bedroom the next morning.

I went back to the apartment where we were staying, and June freaked out and got mad because she was in charge of me and I was only 15. That's when I realized if one night can do this to me—if I'm this stupid one night and I can ruin a lot of things and a lot of trust—that I probably shouldn't drink. It was obviously a problem for me, so that's when I actually got sober.

It's one day at a time, of course, but I hope it stays because I was fortunate enough to figure out what was wrong at a really early age. I think it's because of my mom. It's because I saw what happened to her.

My mom had been sober nine years and had been going to meetings longer than she'd been sober. She'd gone in and out for a while.

I started going to meetings with her when I was seven. I'd do my homework there or just hang out, sleep, whatever. But I know that even though I didn't listen when I was seven, through all the years that I've gone there something got in my head. It's amazing that I even started drinking knowing everything I did, but I was like every other teenager. I think I just wanted to experiment and see if maybe it could work for me. I mean, how do you know you're an alcoholic at 12? You don't. So I wanted to see if I would enjoy it or if I could handle it or what it did for me. I just wanted to experiment, so I did maybe a six- to nine-month period of not even heavy drinking, and that was enough to show me that it didn't work for me, that it would become something worse if I didn't stop at that point. I blacked out every time I drank and it wasn't even that often. I drank mostly on weekends. I threw up almost every time I drank. I would always drink to get drunk, always. I never drank for the taste or to have just a glass. I had as much as what was around me. As much as I could get.

One time, the cops brought me home at two in the morning on a school night. I had been out with my friends, partying at this house where we all wanted to go because it was spooky. Someone had died there, so we thought it was cool for all of us to go and party there. I woke up close to two in the morning on some guy's lap who I didn't know, coming out of a blackout and just freaking out. I didn't know what I was doing.

I had lost a shoe and was walking down the middle of downtown Mill Valley crying, figuring out what I was going to do. It was rainy and miserable. A cop saw me, picked me up and brought me home. The only thing my mom said was, "Well, you know, either you'll sober up or you'll die. It's one way or the other."

She really didn't say too much about my drinking because if she had imposed her views on me and tried to keep me from going out with my friends because I might drink, I think I would have drunk more. I would have rebelled completely. But she just dealt with it and sort of saw it as a normal experimentation that kids go through, and maybe should even go through, to find out if it's right for you or not.

She was pretty much the whole reason I got sober because she gave me a lot of insight on the disease. So did meetings. I just came to my senses and figured out that although I loved alcohol more than anything in the whole world, I should stop because I *did* love it more than anything.

You know, there are a lot of questions people my age ask. I mean, what is there to do? What is left in life after alcohol is taken away from you? Also questions like, "I'm only 19, what am I going to do when I turn 21? How am I not going to go out at night and get drunk? What am I going to do at my wedding or my prom?" But your thoughts change.

My boyfriend and I live together now and we just love to stay home and watch TV and cook dinner. It's the most exciting thing we can think of. Going to a club is less exciting to me, and I'm at the age when I supposedly should be going out and doing that. I'm just not into it. I'm into real simple things now.

I feel good. I feel healthy except for the fact that I smoke cigarettes. Other than that I like not feeling foggy, feeling clear and knowing that alcohol isn't in my system. It doesn't have control over me anymore.

If I hadn't stopped drinking, I wouldn't be where I am today. I wouldn't have the job I have or the boyfriend or the wonderful friends and relationships with my parents and stepparents. Everything is better because my head's clear and I'm more in touch with myself. I really only have me. I realize I only have me and I have to be nice to people. If I find a friend that I really like, I have to give them all I got. I can't imagine where I'd be if I was still drinking.

What really made me want to get sober is I started coming out of denial and realizing that my reality was completely fake. What I thought I was, was fake. What I thought school was, was fake. What I thought friends were, was fake. It's really hard to explain, but I would get drunk like every other alcoholic—to get out of myself and get back into that unreality quick so I wouldn't have to deal with the reality imposing on me. I was trying to find this dreamland and I finally realized it is not the way to live. You can't live this way your whole life. You can't live in this fake world that you're creating in your head; it's being created by alcohol.

I've always looked up to my mom. I think one of the reasons I started drinking, even though I've been going to meetings, was I would always hear these stories of her being real wild when she drank and being real feisty and mouthing off to people. She'd never get hit or no one would talk back to her and she was always the queen of the room. She could say whatever the fuck she wanted to and people let her. So that was kind of glamorous to me. I've always had a foul mouth, too, and we have the same personality—blunt and sarcastic—so I thought I'd like to be the center of attention and do the same things she did.

Most of the times I remember her drunk, she never took it out on me, never hit me or said anything mean to me. It was always fun. Maybe that's why I sort of saw that. I looked up to her because it looked like so much fun. On that same note, she also was an influence on me in the way she got sober, and I looked up to her for that as well. Not only for her drinking, but for the fact that she got sober and realized what was going on.

So it's weird: a lot of my life, the drinking *and* getting sober, has a lot to do with her.

Grace Slick

Grace Slick is a recovering alcoholic and drug addict. She began her successful career as the female lead singer of Jefferson Airplane, one of the top acts of the 1960s and 1970s. The band later changed its name to Jefferson Starship, nailing three consecutive number one hits in the 1980s.

You don't get a little card when you come out that says, "Here's how long this stuff's going to work for you" because it does work for you for a certain period of time, no question about it. Otherwise you wouldn't do it again. Nobody goes out and gets drunk and says, "Boy, that was terrible; I think I'll do it again."

I didn't take China to meetings on purpose. When she was little, I'd go down to the 7-Eleven and she'd say, "Can I go?" She likes to go everywhere. I'm the opposite.

151

I like to stay inside. I mean, you have to put a rocket under my ass to get me up off a chair.

But I assumed that all kids in a situation like hers, where the surroundings are racy or sophisticated, you know, conducive to wrecking yourself—she's around rock 'n' roll stuff, she's around kids who are relatively sophisticated—I assume they're all gonna try something at some point. So I didn't think she was going to go around not drinking or not using drugs. I thought she'd try it, and I had no idea what the result would be. You can't stop anybody, you really can't.

You can train them all you want. There were people on television this morning and they were Christian Scientists. They keep their kids at home, they won't let them go to school because they don't want them to know all these things. They want to teach them how they want them to grow up and with what kind of ideas. And one of them could be an ax murderer—I mean, who knows. I just assumed that whatever happened to her, I'd deal with when it came up.

My grandmother was kind of wild and goofy, and my parents were relatively straight and I'm kind of crazy, so I thought if it's possible it jumps generations, maybe she'll be straight or maybe she'll be a lunatic—I didn't know.

I thought it was outstanding that she realized she had a problem. It takes me forever to realize that something I'm doing probably isn't working for me. Food, chocolate, sugar, alcohol, cigarettes, any kind of behavior that's kind of fun—it's very difficult for me to recognize it myself. Somebody usually has to recognize it for me and to threaten me with all kinds of things before I stop.

I think kids now come and go a lot because they don't have 30 years of destruction behind them. The older you are, the better the chance you're going to stick with it. It's hard for kids to come in at 16 years old and admit they can't drink for the rest of their lives or to believe that six months of negative activity means they're an alcoholic. It's a hard thing to look at.

It's maybe a little easier for China because we know that alcoholism is both genetic and environmental, and she's got a ton of it on both sides of the family, a bunch of wackos. Kids also see the actions that contribute to an alcoholic personality, whereas older people come in because their lives are such a total wreck there's no way they can deny they're alcoholics and they have nowhere else to go. They've lost family, they've lost jobs, they're in the hospital. People think they're nuts, they've got nothing left. Whereas these kids have the rest of their lives. It's harder for them to say, "Yeah, I'm an alcoholic and I'm going to help people and do all the steps and be cool for the rest of my life." That's a tough one.

Unfortunately, you learn a whole lot from really bad situations. I can't say that you don't have fun with drugs and alcohol because I did for 15 years, but you never know who you are. My dad didn't stop until he was 80. I had about 15 or 20 years. China had about six months. Other people have 4½ years, some people have 30. You don't get a little card when you come out that says, "Here's how long this stuff's going to work for you" because it does work for you for a certain period of time, no question about it. Otherwise you wouldn't do it again. Nobody goes out and gets drunk and says, "Boy, that was terrible; I think I'll do it again."

You don't get that little card that says your cutoff date is October 23, 1993, so you always go past the thing. It's not while you're getting loaded and having a good time; it's when you keep going past it, trying to get back that good thing that happened before. It's like jumping out of an airplane with no parachute. Going down is great fun, but when you hit, you're probably not going to look too good.

Telling kids that it's no fun is a lie. It's a lot of fun and very dangerous. It's a real tricky subject because I enjoyed so much of the drug-taking and drinking, but it's easy to say when you're still here. It's easy to say if you're not in a nut house. It's easy for me to say because I didn't go crazy and kill someone. It's real easy for me to say because I didn't hit anybody drunk, I didn't lose my husband or my mind—well, who knows if I lost my mind. Maybe I'm just crazier than shit, I don't know. But it's easier for me to say those things like, "Gee, I had a lot of fun" than it would be for somebody for whom drugs did that thing which is irreparable. In other words, you get so furious you kill somebody while you're drunk. Or go nuts because it gives you wet brain or something like that.

I can't say I didn't enjoy it because I did, but I also didn't have the miserable situation that I could have had. Also, if I kept drinking, who knows where I'd be. I might be sitting around drooling somewhere in a straitjacket.

John Ratzenberger

John Ratzenberger is best known for his role as Cliff Clavin in *Cheers*. He owns a company that produces biodegradable packaging goods, and manages his motion picture and television production company, Atta Boy Productions.

At times it got bad enough
where I'd be over at a friend's house
and my mom, my older sister and my
younger sister in a stroller would come
and get me and we'd get on the bus.
We'd just ride the bus until
he went to sleep.

I don't think you realize other people don't live like this. I think growing up, you assume that when one of your parents comes home at three in the morning drunk and starts a lot of yelling and screaming, that everyone sort of lives this kind of life and that's what reality is. I think children just assume that's the way it is; that's what life is about.

It wasn't until I was well into my adult years that I realized it didn't have to be like that. In the neighborhood where I grew up, I remember going to school one morning and a couple of friends of mine—well, their dad was in the gutter. I literally had to walk around him. He had probably been there all night or just flopped down at four in the morning. He was staggering home from a bar and I guess that's just where he landed.

At least my father didn't spend the night in the gutter, so that sort of brought us up a notch. Now, learning about it, I know it's handed down generation to generation, so in a lot of ways I understand my dad and his drinking habits. There really was no outlet then. There wasn't a recognition of other ways of behaving. But also, during that generation, the whole country had been sucked into the myth of the hard-drinking, hard-fighting cowboy, and that was my father's claim to fame. He was so drunk, the bartender wouldn't serve him and he uprooted the bar and threw the bartender out the door. After he died, his cronies told me stories I never knew back then, but he was the king and nobody messed with him. That was his identity.

Even the guy from whom I copied the character Cliff, same thing: just went out drinking and swaggering with false bravado. It's a lie. His children are all affected by it, every single one of them. Nobody talked about it. All my friends, the people I was with, the same thing was going on with their families. The assumption was *this is it, this is the way it is.* You never believed anyone on television, that's a make-believe world.

I used to watch *Leave It to Beaver* and think it was a comedy because I didn't think that dads went into kids' rooms when they were down in the dumps and said, "What's the matter? What happened?" But now I watch it with a whole new frame of reference because now I know, yeah, it happens. That's what should happen.

About four or five years ago, a buddy of mine sent me some literature and it was astounding. I wept for joy actually knowing I wasn't the only one with all that baggage, finding out that it's not all my fault and that I don't have to continue carrying the baggage along. I don't have to steal my children's childhood like mine was stolen.

When you're in that situation, it makes you very aware, first of all because you don't know whether your parent is drunk, sober, in a good mood, in a bad mood—so you tiptoe, walking on eggs. Any little noise, you're thinking, *What does that mean?* The way the door is closed. Is it a hard close or a soft close? How does he pull into the driveway? What's the lag of time between pulling into the driveway, shutting off the car and getting out of the car? That meant something. At times it got bad enough where I'd be over at a friend's house and my mom, my older sister and my younger sister in a stroller would come and get me and we'd get on the bus. We'd just ride the bus until he went to sleep.

As a child, normally you really want to be playing with your blocks and fooling around with toys; but instead of doing that, your radar is on volume ten, so you've basically lost your childhood. You didn't get a chance to do things like invite the kids over to the house. I thought it was just one of those things: we don't go over to the kids' houses. That's why we meet at a street corner or a ballpark because nobody really wants anybody to come over to the house. We just thought that's the way it was growing up.

Then you realize just how much of your childhood is lost, but that's the nice thing about having kids—realizing—because I spend a lot of time on the rug playing with Legos now. Some of that behavior's going to sneak in. I raised my voice the other night and my son was standing behind me, raising his voice, too, mimicking me. My wife reminded me that children are cameras that never shut off. So they nailed me, they nailed me good, but every now and then you need those reminders.

My father never told me he was proud of me. I think he was. Before he died I talked to him on the phone, when he was in the hospital. He never said it, though. I'm pretty sure he was. My mother told me that he talked about it, but he never said it to me, which is sad. The more I find out about it, the more I find that was very common, especially from that generation.

There's a danger of me overdoing it with my children. If they put a crayon mark across a blank sheet of paper, my instinct is to say I'm so proud of you, isn't that wonderful? But I realize I can't, not every little thing. You want to make sure those words mean something, that's the important thing. So I'm very conscious of growing up without hearing that and making sure I don't say it every day. There's a midpoint somewhere.

Because I grew up in that environment I have to be careful not to get in my own way. I did that a lot. I remember being in Little League and coming home from a game one day and my father said, "'Your uniform's not even dirty, you couldn't have played." My father never came to a game, which was a big disappointment. Maybe then I would have wanted to play, who knows. But the thing that stuck in me was: *my uniform has to be dirty.* Basically, because I was a good kid I didn't just want to roll in the dirt; it had to be legitimate dirt. I was up at bat and I connected with one. I was running and the only thing I could think of was getting my uniform dirty. I didn't know where the ball was. I didn't know if it was an infield fly or a grounder, so I slid into first base. You never slide into first base, but I did because I needed to get my uniform dirty so my dad would be proud of me.

Well, the adrenaline was pumping, I was standing on first base patting my uniform like you see on TV and these people are yelling from the stands and I can't really make out what they're saying until one comes through clearly, a big woman, she's yelling, "Run, you son of a bitch," or something like that. And I said, "What do you mean?" My ball was still in left field. They were still chasing it. I had hit the wall. It came an inch away from being a home run. I got nailed on first because I had to get my uniform dirty.

So when you talk about getting in your own way, that's a prime example. I could have had a stand-up triple or conceivably an in-the-park home run if I would have just kept going and not worried about the baggage, to hit the ball for the sake of hitting the ball for scoring. I was hitting the ball for the sake of getting my uniform dirty, so that my father would be proud of me. It might have been that need for approval that pushed me into acting.

To be a success with a company that makes biodegradable recyclable packing material, that's quite an endeavor. Now that's part of me, and I just keep going. So who knows, without him being like that I may not have achieved what I've achieved. We started out in a garage and we're a big factory now, with forklifts and people with clipboards under their arms checking things off. But if I ended the day in a bar, I'd be sweeping cigarette butts off the loading dock of a company like that instead of owning the damn thing. Booze would have stopped me because I wouldn't have shown up at the right meetings. I wouldn't have seen the opportunity when it was there because I would have been caught up in the alcohol.

Your parents put on you what you are because they are the ultimate authority in your life. If they call you stupid, you're going to be stupid. That's why I make sure that word doesn't exist in our house.

You can say "those stupid shoes" or "those stupid inanimate objects," but it's really hurtful to say that to somebody. I remember sitting in class all through my schooling and the question would be raised and the answer would come right here behind my forehead. I knew exactly what they were talking about and everyone else was struggling with the answer. The teacher would call on Jeremy: "Well, no, that's not it, Jeremy. How about Carol?" And people raised their hands and they didn't know the answer, but I was too afraid to raise my hand because I was stupid, and if the smart kids in class didn't know the answer, then how the hell could I? After all, I've been told I'm stupid.

Also, when you grow up like that—especially coming from a working class background like I did—if you're in an office situation, that means you're in trouble. The principal's office, the boss's office; you're afraid to say something because you think they might yell at you or tell you to get out of the room or laugh at you.

I didn't know anybody who had a desk. I didn't eat at a restaurant with a tablecloth until I was 21. That was intimidating. People with good haircuts and straight teeth were intimidating. So over the years, going to different offices as an actor I'd get angry with myself. Why didn't I just relax enough to say, "This is who I am and this is what I've got for you and nice talking to you, see you later?" It's no big deal.

Now I'm behind a desk with directing and doing all these other things. I know as much as I did when I was 19—instinctively—as far as acting and comedy is concerned. If I only had the courage and wasn't filled with all that nonsense about *this guy's behind a desk so he must know what he's doing.*

I went to England in 1971. Only intended to stay three weeks and ended up staying ten years. It put me in contact with another culture, which I think was very important looking back. It helped me grow up. When you're drinking a lot, the reason you keep on drinking or doing what you're doing is because you have a lot of support. People support you and people make excuses for you. There are people you can borrow money off of. You can always go home and there's going to be something in the refrigerator at your parents' house. Mom is always going to wash your clothes or someone is going to feel sorry enough for you. Someone's going to make excuses for you so that you'll be able to continue being stupid. I couldn't do that anymore. I didn't have anybody. I had to become responsible for myself.

The longer I stayed in England, the stronger I got at being responsible. I was responsible for my actions. You do reap what you sow. All those phrases are so true. That's where I learned that if I said I'd be someplace at a certain time, I better be there because it meant making money. I had nobody to fall back on. That's when I started learning a different way of living.

When I finally got a break in show business, I had to get up at three or four in the morning to be on the set at 7 A.M. because I didn't have a car. I had to take the train to a place and get the bus from that place to go to a location or into the studios. And if I was late, even if I had an insignificant role—one line, which I did, or two lines—the thought of holding people up, that many people just one time looking at their watches waiting for me, that really made me nervous. That's where my nightmares came from.

I also worked as an assistant to a tree surgeon. I was the guy who climbed the trees with all the sharp equipment. There's no way you want to do that with a hangover. If you're a little groggy at that height, you're going to lose something. You're going to come home with fewer digits.

I go back to the old neighborhood and see people I've been close to and see them going through the same thing. Well, there are other ways of behaving. You don't have to do this, but that's frightening, too, because if that's all they've ever known, and that's what's accepted in the eyes of their peers, then where does that leave them?

We all loved my father very much. I still can't be within two miles from where he's buried without stopping my car and crying. I miss him. Again, the information wasn't there back then. Everyone had a secret, a dark secret that you sort of coped with. I wish he was still alive. Maybe he could make his later years a lot happier. I could share with him what I know now.

Chapter IX

LEAP OF FAITH

*If you wanna kiss the sky,
better learn how to kneel.*

—U2
"Mysterious Ways"

Father Leo Booth

Father Leo Booth is a recovering alcoholic. He is a nationally-acclaimed author, lecturer and trainer on all aspects of spirituality and recovery from addictions, and is currently Vicar of St. George's Episcopal Church in Hawthorne, California. He is the author of *The God Game: It's Your Move, When God Becomes a Drug* and *Say Yes to Life.*

I believe that God wants every alcoholic to be recovering, that's his will for us. The tragedy of that is some of us make the connection and some of us don't.

I started to drink when I was 15. I was in a private school in England and they used to give us beer in the evening before we went to sleep. It wasn't so much that I drank the beer to get drunk, it was more the fact

163

that I drank because I liked how I felt when I drank. I drank the beer for effect. It made me feel bigger. When I was a child growing up I had a stutter. When I drank, it was almost like the stutter didn't have any impact. I found a friend in the bottle. This became my power.

I was ordained and was placed in a church in 1971. When you go into a bar dressed as a priest, people notice you and everybody wants to buy a priest a drink. They'd come over and they'd say, "Father Leo, you're the kind of priest we like. God sent you to us. You're not like the others. You're the kind of priest we can relate to."

People started to come from the bars to my church. People used to say, "Shall we stay at home and watch Benny Hill or should we go and listen to Father Leo? The same thing's going to happen." I used to do funny things. I've said this for years, if you're a drunk and you're a truck driver, there will be times when you drive the truck drunk. If you're a priest and you're an alcoholic, there's going to be times you do the service drunk.

I had been drinking and I had a baptism. Mind you that I had performed services and funerals drunk. I had arrived for the baptism and I was feeling mellow. When you're mellow, you don't need any help. I arrived and said, "'Give me the baby." I started to baptize the baby, "In the name of the father and of the son and of the holy spirit, Daphanie!" I didn't ask anybody, I just said, "Daphanie" The mother let loose a scream and she said, "Father Leo, he's a little boy!" I said, "I don't care what the hell it is, it's Daphanie now!" She said, "Is there anything we can do about it?" I said, "No, forever and a day he will be called Daphanie!"

The mother wrote a letter the next day to the bishop. Now a lot of alcoholics can identify with this. The bishop called me after he received the letter and told me he wanted to see me in his office. I'm thinking, *why does the bishop want to see me?* I had forgotten all about the baptism. *Why does the bishop want to see me?* Then I got it—promotion! I go to see the bishop and the bishop says, "I got a letter about you." He asked, "Do you make a habit of baptizing little boys with girls names? Are you sick? Are you demented? Are you having a nervous breakdown? What's the matter with you?"

And then he looks me straight in the eyes, and—all of us alcoholics have heard this from someone—he asked, "Had you been drinking?" He asked it again, "Had you been drinking?" Now see if you can identify with this. I responded, "Who? . . . Me? I swear on the Bible, no."

He didn't believe me, but he couldn't prove it. Have you ever been in that situation when you know that you're telling a lie, and they know you're telling a lie and you know that they know that you're telling a lie, but they can't prove it?

The bishop said, "Quit it, just quit the drink." No mention of a recovery program, just quit it, he said. So I'm driving home and the disease talks to me. The disease says, "Lie low, the bishop's on to you, lie low." I didn't drink for six months. I thought, *I can't be alcoholic if I haven't had a drink for six months.*

If you want to know what's killing alcoholics throughout this world, it's the myths. I didn't drink for six months, therefore I couldn't be an alcoholic. Here's another myth: if you drink beer you're not an alcoholic, or you're not an alcoholic because you don't drink in the morning.

For six months I didn't drink and I didn't think I was an alcoholic. Then one night I went to an engagement party and I do what I've been doing for six months—I drink 7-Up. A lady who used to attend a church where I was a priest years before was at that party and she said, "What are you drinking Father Leo?" I said, "'7-Up." She said, "You used to be gin and tonic." I said, "Now I'm 7-Up." She said, "Have a gin and tonic." I said, "No." She said, "Go on, have a gin and tonic." And I said, "Okay." Just like that. My whole life was about to change. Something extraordinary was about to happen. Then I had another one.

But then something happened. Instead of going off and drinking all night long, I had only two drinks. Remember this disease is cunning, baffling and powerful. It's also very patient. I had two drinks and I went home.

I had washed my hands in the restroom and left my watch in there. The next morning the bartender phoned me and asked if I had lost my watch. "We found it in the restroom," he said. I said, "By the way I had two drinks last night. I'm not supposed to have any." He said, "You were great company last night." I said, "The bishop thinks I'm an alcoholic." He said, "No, you had two drinks, you went home. How can you be an alcoholic?"

I went to get the watch, and the bartender's there. He gives me the watch and then he says, "Have a drink for the road." The night before I had two drinks, but when I took that drink that morning, the lion was disturbed. If you're an alcoholic you know exactly what I mean.

I took a drink and then I took another drink and that lion was disturbed. I knew that I was feeling addiction. Now I set off this demon, this lion, and now I *need* to drink.

I had three drinks there and then I went to another bar, then another bar. I needed to drink like an alcoholic at times needs to drink. At three o'clock in the afternoon I was as drunk as a skunk. I was driving home and my car hit a tree then hit a lamp post and it shot up in the air and crashed on the side of the road. I was bleeding from my leg and my face. I was a mess.

I'm sitting at the side of the road and people were screaming, "Get an ambulance. Get the police." And then I had a spiritual experience.

I'm bleeding and I'm hurt and I'm sitting at the side of the road and I stepped outside of myself and I saw me. I saw me in a way that I've never seen me before. I was now looking at me, from an elevated distance. I saw the crash and I saw the blood and I saw me. And I didn't like what I saw. I didn't want to be that kind of man, that kind of priest. I didn't want to live that kind of life.

There's a moment in all of our lives when suddenly we are confronted with the truth. For me it was the car crash, maybe for other people it was when they turned to their wife whom they love more than anyone else and saw that she's bruised—and they did it. Or maybe when they wanted to be with their children and their children didn't want to have anything to do with them. Maybe for you it's when your mother and father, who brought you into this world, are crying again because of you, because of what you did.

Thank God I can say in my case, I never had a drink again. You know there were moments before that moment, but I never acted on them. I believe if you look at your life, there are many times when God sends down his love and these are precious moments when you see what's really going on. You can reach up and you can hold onto that moment as I've done for 18 years, or you can do what so many people do, and that is forget. God doesn't forget but we can forget. I believe people like us who have had those moments need programs so that we can remember what it was like, what happened, and what's it's like now. We need these spiritual moments when we connect with God, connect with the divine.

The 17th prophecy talks about coincidences of surprise that lead to divine awareness. They appear that they are just coincidences but behind the coincidences is a spiritual truth, and again you must respond to that truth. It's not as if the truth jumps out and hits you on the nose. It's much more that the awareness is there and you are able to see some connection. You need to connect with yourself, with others and with the creation. It starts with really looking at some of these coincidences. There's a kind of divinity that these apparent coincidences in our lives reveal.

You know when I got in my car crash, the faith was there. I'm thinking about David Dodd's example in chapter VI, about how he had a connection when he kept relapsing—a connection with something that is good and wholesome and is more powerful than the addiction—and finally he had a spiritual awakening. In other words he got in touch with the power of God. That connection with the power of God enabled him to realize that no matter how horrible this disease of addiction is, there's a sense in which he can, if he chooses, connect with a power that is more powerful, more health giving, and that's what he did. I suppose that's what I've done and many other people have done. Part of the leap of faith is really connecting with the power that is greater than the disease and greater than the dysfunction that surrounds our lives. It's the willingness on our part to make that connection. And I think that what leads to a successful spiritual recovery is when we're willing to connect with the power that's always there and around us. In many cases we either choose not to respond or not to follow through with it.

It's an ongoing thing, you take the First Step. In my 18 years of recovery, I've gained an understanding about what that unmanageability looks like and more and more about what that powerlessness looks like. I'm sure I'm looking at today very differently than I did when I first got into recovery. Sometimes we forget the disease of alcoholism and addiction is still very much alive. As long as I'm living, there's an alcoholic part of me. If I were to pick up a drink, I would activate that again. I just need to be aware that the steps are not to just get you to a certain place, but the steps are what goes with the tools I use for my ongoing recovery in life.

The aspect of God confuses many people when they enter recovery. They think that God needs to come into their lives. I don't think it's a case of God coming into our lives, I think it's a case that God is already in our lives, that we have to discover God. It's an important difference of emphasis. If you say "God is coming into my life," there's a sense in which you are presupposing that God wasn't there and then he enters. There's a lot of truth in the new age statement, "Wherever you are, God is." I believe that God is there even though in many cases, many of us have a hard time locating God, discovering God or realizing God in our lives. I believe that God showers upon us many, many, many moments of his presence. The leap of faith would be an awareness of God's presence. It's always been there.

Nearly everybody in recovery at some point refers to a moment or to an experience or to an incident that made them see that the world is not an angry, hostile place, that the world is a loving, caring, adventurous experience. Today we can experience life on life's terms.

People need meetings to be able to find the artists in life. The artists in life are always able to find God in almost any situation, that's what makes them special. That's what makes people who are positive and creative. My definition of spirituality is being a positive and creative person. That's because I believe that God is positive and creative. People that come to meetings need to sit and listen to people who have a positive and creative attitude towards life. You need to learn how to do it: it's the art of learning spiritual life.

There are always people who are out there who can basically answer some of the problems that you are experiencing in your life, and you have to go searching to find them. When you find them, be prepared to listen to what they have to say.

Things are only going to change when you change them. If you keep doing and thinking the same things, you will keep receiving the same results. If you want different results for what's going on in your life, you must do things differently, be willing to think differently about things.

That's why they suggest you go to so many meetings in the beginning. It's just getting people into a ritual. Take the alcoholic and drug addict. They have a ritual around their drug use. They have a ritual around their drinking. They drink in a certain bar, they usually drink a certain drink, they usually drink with certain people and certain times of the day. In a similar way we need to create healthy rituals that are going to bring about our spiritual recovery.

I think it's important to get into the ritual of calling a sponsor, somebody who you believe has wisdom and recovery, and somebody with whom you want to connect. I think you need to do it on a regular basis. I think you need to substitute recovery experiences and recovery happenings in your life for the kind of drug ritual or alcohol ritual that you used to perform for many years. And I also think a very important part of the spiritual journey is to be patient with yourself. Sometimes you want all recovery right away. You have to be willing to progress within the process: progression within the process. You will not get recovery in just 90 days, but the 90 days are going to establish for you a method of living, a method of facing your day, a method of treating your alcoholism. That method will lead to ongoing recovery.

You develop a healthy relationship with God once you start to have a healthy relationship and respect for yourself. By knowing who you are, you will discover who God is. In other words, the way to discover the handiwork of God in our lives is to really spend time examining what's going on in our lives, to really get to know yourself. Jesus said, "Love God and love your neighbor as yourself." In the process of loving yourself, you get to understand your neighbor. You also get to understand God. That's the key to developing a healthy relationship with God.

I think when you use the term, "Let go and let God," what people need to realize is this God power that plans everything in your life and makes everything run smoothly is not going to just take over. One of the things that you find early in recovery is that there's a daily responsibility that you have in life, and you also have a daily responsibility in regard to creating and sustaining your relationship with God. You need to really look at the prayers that you say. I encourage people to write their own prayers. You need to say your prayers really every morning and evening because morning is the time when you start your day and the evening is when you can thank God for what has happened in your day. It's so easy to forget and not say you're prayers because you're so busy having relationships with everybody on the planet. That morning time with God and that evening time with God is very special. It keeps you mindful of what's been going on in your life.

I'm so grateful that the 12-Step program doesn't say in its 12th Step, having had a *religious* awakening. It doesn't say that, it says having had a *spiritual* awakening. I believe that religion and spirituality are not the same. Somebody said it so beautifully in this program, "Religion is man-made, spirituality is God-given." Religion can divide people up—I'm Jewish, I'm a Muslim, I'm a Hindu. Spirituality teaches the world to hold hands.

I believe that God wants every alcoholic to be recovering, that's his will for us. The tragedy of that is some of us make that connection and some of us don't. I've always been intrigued, how is it that some of us get well and some don't? Some seem to struggle forever and others seem to find recovery very easy. What's the difference? I think the difference is the willingness that some of us have to make the connection on a daily basis with a power that's greater than ourselves.

Most people who relapse are usually people who for years have made the connection and then get lazy, they detach from a recovery program or recovery people and they forget from where they came. It's a dangerous and slippery place if you don't make a connection with your higher power on a daily basis. You can easily go back to the behavior that you either denied or have forgotten. Look how the Jews view the Holocaust, they constantly want to remember what it was like so that they don't allow that behavior to erupt in our society again. In a way, we're dealing with an alcoholic Holocaust, and if we don't choose to remember it, it can all come back.

John Hiatt

John Hiatt is a recovering alcoholic and drug addict. In addition to releasing several successful solo albums, he's written songs for numerous country and rock artists, including Bonnie Raitt, John Doe and Iggy Pop.

God didn't let me turn from liquor and drugs until I got to the point where I had just a little more faith that there was another alternative than I had faith in the alcohol and drugs. That's when the moment of clarity hit.

I was in a marriage that had completely fallen apart through years of my carrying on with other women and drinking and drugging. I had a daughter who was about three months old. I was estranged from my wife at the time. I had finished an album and was involved with another woman.

I was driving around Mississippi in a black Camaro with this other woman, this Dutch girl, and drinking and snorting cocaine. I couldn't get drunk and I couldn't get sober. I couldn't stop crying. I thought I was going to die. I thought my heart was going to blow up. It was the end. I was crashing and burning. All of a sudden there was a little moment of clarity. I had been to a psychiatrist about four months before and of course, as we alcoholics are prone to do, I never shot straight with the guy. You know: "How much did you drink?" "Oh, not much at all."

After about a month of seeing me, he apparently had just about enough of my bullshit and he told me point-blank, "Look, I can't help you." That made me mad. "What do you mean you can't help me? One hundred bucks an hour!" He said, "What you need is to go to a treatment center." Naturally, I disagreed. Then I stormed out of his office.

But there in Mississippi, somewhere around Biloxi I think it was, in that black Camaro of death, as I now refer to it, it was like that little light bulb. I heard his voice say that. "I can't help you. You need to go to a treatment center." Ultimately, he helped me immensely just by planting that seed. That's a power greater than myself working in my life. I didn't know it at the time, but I choose to see it that way now. That was the beginning of recovery for me. I went back to Los Angeles and went into a 28-day treatment center.

I resisted at first. I resented the people and all the recovery talk and higher powers. I don't want to assign this to a particular program because as you know, I can't affiliate myself or speak for a particular 12-Step program. But in general recovery terms, there was talk about a power greater than ourselves. I was completely uncomfortable and skeptical of the whole thing. I thought these people were jerks, but I was whipped. It's an unfortunate failure of the disease that it has to kick your butt before you're willing to reach out. At least that's how it was in my case. I hate to think that everybody has to go to the wall because some people don't make it back. In fact, a lot don't. This is what we're dealing with. It's a powerful disease.

The treatment center afforded me the opportunity to stop spinning my wheels. My lifestyle was such that I had been going in this same cycle for years—making albums, touring, drugs, alcohol, women—just crazy behavior. That was my life. For the first time I was able to just sit still for a moment. I began to feel. Somewhere I knew that I didn't have a choice anymore. I knew I had to get some help. That's really what it was. I knew I needed help for the first time.

I stayed in the treatment center for 28 days because I was afraid of the alternative. I knew that the only thing out there waiting for me was destruction and, eventually, death. I really didn't see any other way around it. That's how hard-headed this disease is. That's how it works. That's what kind of hold it has.

I had my first brush with a spiritual kind of awakening experience right around three months. It was simply realizing one day that I had stayed clean and sober for three months. I had never been able to do that in my life. I knew that something else was at work here. It wasn't just me doing it. It was a marvelous feeling. I wasn't alone. It was clear to me that something was taking place that was not my doing, that some power was at work here. It was a wonderful feeling. It was the first time I really felt like I was a part of something.

At six months I had to go to work. We had a European tour booked. It would be my first sober tour. Since I was a kid, I had never played in front of people without the benefit of a mind-altering chemical. So it was scary as hell, but somehow I was able to focus on my recovery and put that first. Somehow I knew that was the important thing—to stay sober.

Looking back on it, I guess, through the grace of God, I had my priorities somewhat straight. I was asking this power greater than myself every step of the way, "Look, if I can't do this and not drink, then I'll come home." That was kind of the deal I made because that's how important it was for me to stay sober.

So what happened, and it was not comfortable, I won't kid you, I was up on stage and I would be singing a song and my mind would be racing. I would be talking to myself and my head was going, *You're a fake, you're a phony, what are you doing up here? This is bullshit, you never even liked music. Who are you kidding?* All of that. The committee in my head, while I was singing: the first couple of weeks it was hard as hell and I was uncomfortable. I was in Europe on a tour and that's a special situation. It's hard to catch a meeting on a tour because your day is so structured. Most of your time is spoken for. It's trickier to find an English-speaking meeting when you're in a different country every day. It was scary but I got enough meetings to get me through. I just prayed my butt off and something happened. It was a five-week tour and about three weeks into it, all of a sudden I found myself remembering what a neat thing music was. That's how far off the track I was. I got so caught up in the sideshow—the drinking and the drugs, the partying and all this crazy stuff—that the whole reason, the whole thing I'd loved initially, which was just the thrill and the moving, the pleasure and the emotions of music, I had lost touch with. It was almost like God was giving it back to me. It's like, when I was willing to give it up—if it meant I couldn't stay sober—I got it back. It was the first clear-cut example of just let it go and it'll work out.

It was beautiful. The last two weeks of the tour, I had a ball just making this music. It was wonderful. That was the beginning. I knew pretty much from that point on that I was going to be okay with this line of work, that I could do this.

On that tour, we had to do an appearance in a record store in Holland. Some guy I had known from a previous tour was there. He walked up to me and shook my hand and left a packet of cocaine in my hand. I jumped about 10 feet in the air because I knew this was life and death stuff to me. I took my road manager aside and said, "Come here, you have to help me." I ran into the other room and said, "You have to take this right now. Take it out of my hand." It's like I was holding a grenade or something.

Today, I really don't have the problem of wanting to have a drug or a drink on a daily basis. I have plenty of other problems and I know that I've got the same sick behavior. If I let it run amuck and don't use the tools given to me to stay in recovery, eventually it will lead back there. I don't know how long it will take, but I do know it will be much worse.

Meetings are my lifeline. I have to connect with the recovering community regularly because the disease forgets. It's a disease that tells you you don't have it. Before you know it, you're off and running. I haven't learned anything in recovery that didn't take me hitting the wall. That's the way I learned. It just seems that my disease is of the type that I have to push things to the limit before I can let go of them.

One big feature of recovery is that it gives me options. It's all designed to make my life simpler, easier and better. This power greater than myself really loves me and cares for me so much that it doesn't want me to be miserable. I make my own misery when I blow up and let that anger out with my friends and family. They, of course, get hurt feelings and it comes back on me. It hurts me, so I'm trying to develop other ways that don't hurt me to get the anger out. I've been able to unload some of my anger in various ways. I went through some co-dependency therapy, going back to some issues from my childhood, checking into that kind of stuff. I learned to deal with my father's death. Liquor and drug abuse simply puts off our emotions. The whole reason we pick up this shit to begin with is because life is just too emotionally painful. At least it was for me. Alcohol and drugs saved my life. That's another irony of the disease. I mean, if I hadn't picked up a drink or a drug, I think I might have blown my brains out.

I heard a guy in the program—and it took me a while to understand this, but I think it's a beautiful thing today—he said denial is a gift from God. God didn't let me turn from liquor and drugs until I got to the point where I had just a little more faith that there was an alternative than I had faith in the alcohol and drugs. That's when the moment of clarity hit. That's exactly what it was. I wouldn't have thought about what that psychiatrist said if I hadn't believed that, in fact, there was some help for this problem.

I'm starting to learn about this creature named John Hiatt. I amaze myself with what I am able to do. Every day is really an adventure and I'll tell you, I have a life today. They talk about living beyond your wildest dreams. It really is like that. I could never have imagined living the kind of life I'm living today, with friends and people I really care about and who really care about me. I feel a part of a community. I feel like a human being.

Prayer is a wonderful thing. I'll be involved in a project and have to leave the room and say the serenity prayer because I feel the anger, that old stuff that doesn't really have anything to do with the situation, and I recognize it now. I feel it welling up and I don't want it. My main thing today is to just try to suit up, show up and stay out of trouble. I know that I make my own trouble.

I heard a guy early on say acceptance means approval, and I liked that because I can accept the way things are today. I can try. That's all I can do. Some days I accept it better than others, but I can accept, for instance, that I may be in a situation in a given time with some people I'd rather not be with. I can accept the fact that they're the way they are. Doesn't mean I have to like the way they are. But I can deal with it and take care of myself in that situation. That's something I couldn't do before I stopped using.

You know, all you have is one day, one day at a time. That's also a hard thing. I don't want to sit here and tell you that I've got that down pat because I don't. I mean, part of my disease is that I'm always anywhere but where my body actually is. I'm either back in the past bemoaning something I did or something that was done to me, or I'm off somewhere in the future trying to figure things out. My will, self-will run riot. The hardest thing for me to do as an addict and alcoholic is to accept life on life's terms a day at a time. That's the nut. That's the nut that I intend to crack.

What I got today that I didn't have before recovery is the willingness to try to deal with this concept of a day at a time. You only have to not drink and do drugs for 24 hours. If it's really hard, you break it down to hours or minutes. I did that. I still do sometimes. I don't have a desire to drink or take drugs today, but I've got all kinds of other crazy behavior. I can get addicted. I can abuse people, places and things. It's like, what do you have? That's my disease. I have it and it's just not ever going to go away. But I have a way with dealing with it today. What sobriety's done is allow me to attempt to live a successful life a day at a time. That takes place on all sorts of different levels. Before sobriety, I thought success was being loved, worshipped and adored by millions and millions of fans, and selling zillions of records. That was basically it. There was nothing that could fill that hole, that hole in my gut. Today there is something that can fill that hole. It's amazing.

Mike Binder

Mike Binder is a recovering alcoholic and drug addict. He began his career as a stand-up comedian and has continued writing and directing motion pictures, which include *Coupe de Ville, Indian Summer* and *The Bridge.*

One of the things that meetings taught me was to have all these people in my life. The closer these relationships are, the closer I am to God. It's really an awesome thing to comprehend and come to.

I lived in a lot of fear. I was one of those guys who always wanted to get ahead and do the things I wanted to do, but I was always afraid I wasn't good enough. I was always fooling everybody. It was one of those situations, looking back on it now, where the fear was greater than the reality. Being high and drunk and being a drug user was something that helped me mask that fear.

177

Not only was it a way to be easy around other people in a social environment, but it was a way to calm that inner voice telling me I was a phony and I was no good, that I lacked certain skills other comedians and writers had. What it was really doing was amplifying that voice. I didn't realize that. It was holding me back.

The last time I did drugs I was filming the *Detroit Comedy Jam*. I had been sober all through the production and the filming. The night after the filming, I got high on cocaine. It's like I had all this energy and drive to get the project done, a long project that I had been working on for quite a few years. It was like a dream come true. All of the sudden I was doing cocaine and grass again, and all through the editing process I was absent. I would find reasons not to be there. I would go off and do nightclub jobs. I really should have been there in the editing room, paying attention. As it worked out, we had a great producer, Bill Pace, who kind of covered for me. He didn't realize what I was doing to myself. Here I was on the threshold of a dream, and I was running away from it, taking drugs.

When I went out to L.A., I had 15 grams of cocaine, a huge bag of pot and a cooler full of rum and Coke. I got halfway out there, and it was the greatest thrill in the world, with the drugs and driving, just zonked out, out of my mind. I'm surprised I didn't kill someone. When I got to Colorado, a snowstorm hit at the same time all the drugs and the booze ended, or were gone, and the last part of the trip was the longest, cruelest, most depressing drive in history. I got to L.A. and I thought, *I have to do something, I have to get some help.* I kept refusing to get help.

I was in the Comedy Store and I asked a comedian named Jesse, who's a wonderful guy, for a joint. He's helped a lot of comedians get sober. He was really one of the first of the young comedians to get sober. I asked him for a joint, and he goes, "Boy, you're in bad shape." I said, "Yeah, I just need a joint to calm down," and he said, "No, you don't need a joint. You need some help. Why don't you go to a meeting?" I said, "No, I don't want to go, Jesse." He gave me the address of a meeting and said, "Meet me there tomorrow night. It'll do you a lot more good than me giving you a joint."

I went to that meeting the next night and I heard people saying things—I hated it by the way, my first meeting—but I heard people saying things that rang true to me.

You know, I was at a meeting the other day and a newcomer said,

"I don't know how I'm going to spend the rest of my life not drinking. I'm not going to have fun anymore." That's how I was at my first meeting. I used to say to the guys, "I feel like the rest of my life's going to be so dull without drugs and alcohol." And they would say, "Well, don't worry about the rest of your life, worry about today; just deal in this 24-hour increment. You don't know what the rest of your life will be like without drugs and alcohol. Just make the commitment that today you won't take any blow or you won't drink."

Now I have more fun than I ever did. One of the reasons is—and I think this is really important, I always try to talk to newcomers about this—the reason I needed drugs and alcohol to have fun was because people around me were people who only had fun with drugs and alcohol. When I changed my life, I changed the circles I moved in, and the people I'm with now don't need drugs and alcohol to have fun.

I'm very protective of my sobriety, very, very protective. One thing I don't do is let people too far into my life who do drugs and alcohol. I'm not rude to them. If I'm at a party and someone lights up a joint, that's fine. But for the most part, I don't have people over for dinner that are drug users. I don't go to a house where I know there's going to be a lot of dope. For the most part, I stay around people that live clean lives. I find those people pick me up. People who use drugs and alcohol pull me down.

I have a friend whom I love, one of my oldest friends, who called me up and wanted to visit me here in California and stay for a week. Actually, two of them were going to come, and then he called and said the other guy couldn't come and he was going to come alone. I had to say no because in spite of the fact that I love the guy I couldn't afford to be around him, just me and him hanging out for a week in L.A. at night. I know he uses drugs and alcohol, and I feel that when I'm in the company of a practicing alcoholic or drug user—not saying a casual drug user, but someone that's a drug abuser—I'm too protective of my sobriety. I stay away from that.

When you're using, you think you're such close friends. I had a couple of friends—one in particular, who is a very famous comedian. When I got sober, he used to say to me, "Michael, come back out, get off the wagon. I liked you better when you were using drugs. You were funnier." He would always say that to me. "You were funnier when you were on drugs, man. You were funnier high." I realized it wasn't that he thought I was funny; it was that he didn't like me getting sober. He was threatened by the fact that I was cleaning up my life and he wasn't. He was doing everything he could to pull me back down. And that was my big fear: that I wasn't going to be funny anymore.

The truth of the matter is that a lot of my friends who were drug users were really threatened by me getting sober. The ones who were my true friends have since become sober. But when you've got a friend who's telling you, "Come on over and get high with me," or you're trying to clean up your act and they're tempting you with a joint or with a line of coke, they're not your friend anyway, so you have nothing to lose. That was my big thing. I've always been really into my friends. I've always been a guy who's had a lot of buddies, and my whole fear was that I wouldn't be in with my buddies. Now most of the buddies I thought were close aren't close at all. We had drugs in common and that was about it.

The people I know now, whom I've met in the course of being sober and leading a clean life, they are my true friends. If I need them in the middle of the night, they'll get out of bed and come. If I need money or a shoulder to cry on, if I need to get picked up, if my wife is sick and I need some help, they'll be there.

Sometimes when I go to a meeting and I look around the room and I realize I've known these people for years, that I've seen them go through their ups and downs, I realize how much I care about them. My eyes water, I fill up with emotion. I realize I really truly care for these people. I really care about who they are and how their lives are progressing. I don't think I cared about people before.

My parents divorced when I was very young. They were both into their own trips. I went off on my own and went to Hollywood to make it big. I just wanted to make it big for myself. For the most part I pretended to be a caring guy, but I really didn't care about anyone but myself. I think I was running through the drugs and the alcohol. Since I've sobered up, I've been learning to really care about people. Relationships in your life make you realize how rich life is. I care about people much, much more.

I have friends who call me and ask, "Can we take a walk tonight?" And when I'm out there on this walk, I realize there's a real bond between us. I really feel for this person. That's the one thing I'm really growing into. That's something that's a part of my life that I never really had. I have these really wonderful relationships. I'm kind of learning that we can get God through each other, get God and give God, through each other. One of the things that meetings taught me was to have all these people in my life. The closer these relationships are, the closer I am to God. It's an awesome thing to comprehend and come to.

I was with a friend the other night and it struck me that we're not that close. We've been friends for years and years and we tell everyone that we're best friends, but we're not all that close. We talk about our careers. We talk *at* each other instead of *to* each other. People I know in recovery, I talk with. I hear them. I feel them. It's a whole different level. It comes from that pain, that joint pain we've been through, that we're in. We're recovering from a disease and we're also on a spiritual path together. I'm here today. Life's in session. This isn't a dress rehearsal, that's what I'm learning.

This is it and to worry that I can't ever smoke pot or do cocaine . . . you know, the truth of the matter is, I don't care. I probably will never take drugs again. The clean life is wonderful. I'm not a drug user, I'm a recovering drug addict. I don't take drugs and I don't take alcohol. It's part of my life I don't need. Gaining that for the rest of my life is more important than knowing I can never again get high.

This country's at war in the streets with each other over drugs and alcohol. We get murdered and families are coming apart. I have the pride of knowing I'm not part of that. I'm not contributing to that. In fact, I'm just the opposite. I'm the other side of that. I'm the good side.

I never stood for anything in my life. I stood for me, Mike Binder. I wanted to get out of Detroit and make it big and be cool and be on the cover of *People Magazine* and be looked up at. Those were my principles. Those were my values. Now I have something I stand for. I stand for clean living. I want people to know that. I want people in my family—my little cousins, people down the hall in my building—to know *this guy's clean.* I stand for something. I'm a symbol for something. That means a lot to me. You know my parents never wonder, *Is he in trouble? Did he go off and get drunk?* They know I live a clean life. So when I go into the future and think 60 years ahead, I think, *Well, hey, I'm going to be sober for the rest of my life. That's cool.*

The story of *Coupe de Ville* is a miraculous one. I was sober six months and had been writing a lot of comedies that were just comedies that made money. I thought everyone wanted to see these dumb *Police Academy* comedies and things like that.

I had this bad taste in my mouth about writing and the work I was doing on stage. I got on my knees one morning and I asked God to help me write something worthwhile, to help me write something with heart that's about something. About an hour later, my step-mother, Jean, who's a real important voice in my life, called. She said to me, "You know, your dad and his two brothers were here last night and they went over that Cadillac story. That's the movie you should write. You always say you're going to write a movie, write that one."

When I hung up the phone, it occurred to me what an omen it was. I had just been down on my knees praying for a sign of something to write, and for the first time I saw it as a piece about love, a piece about unity. When I attacked it from that angle, about the warmth between family members and the love that's there even in the tough times, the piece came together and people started becoming interested.

So I've always looked at *Coupe de Ville* as a gift of my sobriety. The material I've written since then, the stuff I'm working on now is much warmer. I was not a warm comedian. People think of me now and say, "Oh, he's very warm." I hear that all the time. During my last HBO special I ended with this very sweet piece, and I always hear people describe me like that. But I was *never* a warm comedian before. I was always this wild, smart-ass punk kid who swore and spit on the audience, and here I am getting sober and all this warmth comes out and I'm writing all these screenplays that have so much heart to them, and people respond to that. People respond to that side of me. They didn't respond to the dark side of me. I find that the warmth sobriety has added to my life has really helped my work. So that's the major thing. I think *Coupe de Ville* was the first inkling of that.

When you're sober, you can look at yourself much better. When you do comedy that comes from your soul and your gut, it's advisable not to be too screwed up on something so you can hear the voice in your gut telling you what to write.

Here's the difference: When I used to write, I'd get a mound of coke, a bag of pot and a bottle of rum and I would stay up all night. I would play the Comedy Store, and I would leave and I'd write and balance that coke and that pot and the rum until about eight in the morning. Then I'd crash out. But I'd be up all night writing and I'd write a scene, and then I'd roll a joint and then do a line and I'd have a drink, and I'd get ready and do another scene.

Now I write early in the morning. Before I write I get on my knees and I say, "God, open me up to be an instrument of your work. Show me what to write, help me write something that's about something, and guide me to where you want to take me as a writer. I'm your tool." In between scenes sometimes I stop and I get back down on my knees again. The days I do that are the days the best stuff comes out. The best scenes, the best stuff that people remember from *Coupe de Ville,* the stuff that people quote from other movies—it's always the stuff that I got right after stopping and taking a prayer break, which blows my mind. It feels silly saying that. I was never someone who said, "Hey, man, want to write a great script? Pray." But that's where I'm at now and that's what sobriety has done for me.

I knew my wife long before I was in recovery. She was the manager at my bank and I hated her. She was always mad at me because I was writing bad checks to coke dealers. Then I saw her, years later, at a meeting. I found out she had been in recovery for a few years and we became good friends. I was breaking up with another girl-friend—we had come through a rocky relationship—and Diane and I went for coffee and talked about it. I had no idea she'd be my wife. I said things to her that I would never tell my future wife. We just became really good friends and we went to meetings together and I was able to open up to her in such a way that she saw another whole side of me. I wasn't trying to impress her. I was showing her vulner-ability that I'd never really shown anyone, and that's what she fell in love with. As far as our day-to-day relationship, not only is it the longest relationship in my life, but I think Diane knows me better than anyone has ever known me. I know recovery has made me much more accepting of her as a human being. I'm much more willing to just take her as she is and worry about myself and not worry about her. I didn't think that would happen in a love relationship or a mar-riage. We really work a program in our marriage and we take it one day at a time. There's a lot of talking and a lot of communication, even in the rough times. I never thought I'd say it, but I have a mar-riage that works. People around me know that. My wife and I both know that. It's a gift of recovery and it's because of recovery that we do everything we can to make sure we don't spoil it, even though I screw up a lot or come close to blowing it. I think the real thing is you have to get to a point where you get these gifts in your life and you realize you didn't do them. They were gifts from God. You don't want to give them back. You hold onto them.

Sobriety's a gift from God, nothing else. When you get a gift from

God like clean living, you hold onto it like there's no tomorrow. You get a gift like a good wife and a good marriage and a supportive relationship, you hold onto it, do whatever you can. It's like with work—you hold onto it and remember all the time that it's God doing it.

Last Friday, Twentieth Century Fox put a script I was working on for three years into turnaround, a piece about my summer camp (*Indian Summer*), a very real piece about my own childhood. They abandoned it. I was able to say, "Hey, that's fine, it'll work out. It's God's plan. It's not my time, it's God's time. God has a better plan for that script than having Fox make it right now." People are calling me saying, "Oh, sorry to hear this," but I was fine with it.

In the old days I would go off on a five-day binge. I would go off on a binge and get loaded, whining, "Poor me. Everyone's doing better than me. I can't get a break." Now it's not a big deal. There are no big deals when you're sober.

It's really incredible and that's what you learn. I go to this men's luncheon five days a week in Santa Monica and we just sit around, guys in recovery, and there are guys who have been there for 30 years, guys 10 years, guys 2 days, guys a day, and we sit around and talk about our lives. We go around and have our hamburgers and our salads and we talk about our lives. You come to realize that we're enough, if we can just get out of our own way. We have plenty. We have everything we need and all of our dreams can come true. It's just a matter of getting out of our own way.

I think the greatest revelation for me is when you do an inventory and you look down to all your inner thoughts and resentments, and who you are, and you tell it to someone else and they say, "Yeah, I feel the same way." You had all these dark secrets, then you find someone else with the same ideas. If you stick around meetings long enough, you realize that everybody thinks the same way you do. All these things I think—that I was a loser, I wasn't good enough—everybody thinks that.

God is in my life every day. First thing in the morning, I get out of bed and on my knees and I thank God for another day. I ask him to help me make the most of my day and be the best Mike that I can be. I ask him to show me how I can serve him and be an instrument of love. It sounds so corny talking about it. I was never that type of person. I was the person ten years ago who'd say, "Yeah, here's your instrument of love [grabs himself]." That's not how I am now. I believe in that.

I'm living a normal life with God at the center. It's really wonderful and I don't shy away from it. I'm not embarrassed by it and anybody that scares, that's their problem. It's what makes my life great.

Chapter X

PLAYING IT STRAIGHT

God, grant me the serenity
To accept the things I cannot change,
The courage to change the things I can,
And the wisdom to know the difference.

—Reinhold Niebuhr

Wayne Dyer

Wayne Dyer is the author of several bestselling books and audio programs including *Your Sacred Self, Real Magic, You'll See It When You Believe It* and *Your Erroneous Zones.* His books have been translated into over 45 different languages around the globe.

If you're thinking about quitting, you're doing it, which is great. If you're thinking about it and not doing it, don't get down on yourself. Everything starts with a thought. The ancestor to every action is a thought.

I think the first thing you get with sobriety is more hours in the day. If you have two or three beers in the evening, the rest of the night is shot because you get sleepy. I've gained a lot more alertness in my life and probably an extra four or five hours a day to live because I sleep much less now than I used to. I'd fall asleep in the evening or just get drowsy. I don't do that any more.

189

My relationship with my wife has also dramatically improved because it was a sore spot that I would drink in the evening. She didn't trust me when I used anything or when I drank because it changes your judgment. I have much better judgment now about what I can and can't do, and what I want to do in my life.

I've also become closer to God; I feel much more of a spiritual base. I am "high" a lot more. I feel a lot higher. I feel higher on life. Whatever it was that I was looking for in those substances and drinking, I've learned how to achieve those feelings without it. So the idea that being high is bad doesn't work for me. I think it's great.

I do it through meditation. I can get that euphoric, giddy, high, wonderful, light feeling without any toxicity. It's not a counterfeit freedom. I've achieved more freedom. The freedom you get from drinking is counterfeit because you always have to get more; you're always looking for more of it, whereas the freedom that you get from a natural high doesn't require that you keep constantly refurbishing yourself. It's always there.

I had a teacher explain to me that if you really want to know higher awareness, you have to experience sobriety. I remember Castaneda's early works talked about doing mushrooms and so on, peyote, and his teacher then told him that he couldn't do that anymore, that he had just introduced him to those things so that he would know that there was another dimension and that it was accessible. Then he was going to teach him how to get there without killing himself. It was like an introduction to a higher dimension. If you are poisoning your body or your brain with substances, you can't use them to reach the highest state of awareness.

Judgment has a lot to do with it, too. Sobriety greatly affects your judgment. All you have to remember is that when you judge someone or something, you don't define that person or thing with your judgment—you define yourself. You don't get the privilege of defining another human being with your judgment. Calling someone else a jerk or whatever doesn't make that person a jerk; it means that you need to put those kinds of labels on other people. So you really define yourself. That's why Jesus said, "Judge not," because when you do you're really just saying something about yourself.

If you're thinking about quitting, you're doing it, which is great. If you're thinking about it and not doing it, don't get down on yourself. Everything starts with a thought. The ancestor to every action is a thought. I thought about not drinking for 10 years. You have to understand: I never had a DUI, I was never drunk, I was never stumbling around. I could be in the middle of a beer and walk away from it. I didn't have the typical alcoholic symptoms that most alcoholics have, but I did drink every day and I recognized that that's alcoholic behavior. But it wasn't out-of-control behavior at all. However, it was playing too much of a role in my life.

I started thinking, *How long has it been since I haven't had a beer in the evening?* And it had been probably ten years since I hadn't had at least one beer in the evening. I don't think I ever had more than three a night in my life, but I had it every day. Then I thought, *I'm going to have a day when I don't do it,* and I would really work on it. It would get to be six or seven o'clock and I would have my meal and right away the beer would be there. But then the time came.

See, it's like you have to think about things and put them in the invisible dimension for a long time. It's like quitting smoking or anything: if you're thinking about it, you're doing it. Thinking's just the beginning of the process. So be grateful that you're thinking about it. Give yourself a pat on the back for thinking about it. Don't put yourself down because you're just thinking about it and not doing it. If you think about it enough, what you think about is what expands. As you think, so shall you be. Think about it, think about it, think about it . . . and eventually it will become automatic.

Think of the word "form." Put the word out there and then see what happens when you put the word "in" before it, like when you're informed, that's "in-form-ation." Now, "ation" means the result or experience of. So now we've got a word—"information," the result or experience of being informed. All of the information that you get in your life—from others, from books, from everything—is all the ego. It's the stuff that keeps you rooted exclusively in form.

Then get rid of the "in" and put "trans" in place of it. Now you have a new word, "transformation," which means the result or experience of going beyond your form—that's the higher self, that's the sacred self. When you transform your life, you go beyond your form, you leave your form behind and you become the witness.

When you do this, practice cultivating the witness—mentally challenging some of the ideas that keep you from having a blissful life—and begin to even question whether or not the physical world is something that you have to stay stuck on. Consider the words of

Christ: "Even the least among you can do all that I have done and even greater things." Do those words ring true for you? Do you have the divine capacity? Are you willing to claim your power? All you have to do is have a daily affirmation that says, "I am willing to claim the power, the divineness that I am." But you can't do that when you're in the world of limits, which is what the world of form is.

I always like the quote by Blaise Pascal that I used in *Real Magic.* He says, "All of man's troubles stem from his inability to sit quietly in a room alone." If you learn how to do that and take time to do that, you will see changes immediately.

Generally when you're drinking, especially in an alcoholic fashion, you don't have the time nor do you want to make the time to improve your life, let alone your consciousness. Meditating is one of the furthest things from your mind. Quiet time does not just happen.

One of the things I've learned is to get up early in the morning, between three and six, and force myself out: get out of the paradigm that I have to stay in bed. Go out there and walk and run in that quiet time of the day. Most of the answers that I seek in my life, I will find. I get closer to God all the time.

You need to tap into your higher awareness. That's what *Your Sacred Self* is all about. It's really understanding the phenomenon of knowing that there's two of us in every body. One of us is this ego, which is just an idea we have that is rooted in the physical world that we are special—important—and we are easily offended. It's what I call being under the spell of matter, of materialism, of everything we experience in the world—that which is noticed. But then there is the noticer. The noticer is the part of us that is invisible and is the cause of everything in the material world. And it's just so simple. If we could learn somehow to just sort of oscillate between the physical world, the material world and the spiritual world—if we could just learn how to get in there—we could really take charge of what we call the mechanics of creation. We could begin to create what we want for ourselves in our lives because everything in the material world has a cause in an unseen dimension. The same thing is true of our lives.

What we've done is forfeited our ability to go back and forth between these worlds. We just are under the spell of matter, under the spell of that which we see rather than under the spell of the seer, or the noticer. All I'm trying to teach people is how to get in there and know that you can really manage the coincidences of your life when you do that. See, you are all those things at all times. You are the noticer and you are that which you notice, and you can't escape that. It's just that your belief is that you're only that which you experience with your senses.

You also have to remind yourself that if you make something difficult and tell yourself you're going to have trouble doing it, then you've already determined what the outcome is going to be. I think the seven most important little words ever strung together are: "As you think, so shall you be." If you understand that, what you think about is what expands. If you just have a tiny little doubt about your ability to get quiet and get peaceful and know the sacred within you, then you'll act upon that doubt. Remember, the ancestor to every action is a thought. So begin to challenge the kind of thoughts you have. Give yourself time, even if you sit there and wonder, *What am I doing here?* Just give yourself 20 minutes.

I used to do that before I learned to meditate, when I was a college professor and I had a practice. I had a million things going on. I'd be in my office and it would be just turmoil everywhere. People would be waiting for me, the phones would be ringing, that kind of scene. I would just excuse myself and I'd tell them I'd be back in 15 minutes, that I had a very important engagement. It was an engagement with God. I would just walk out of the building and go to a park a block away. I would sit on a bench, get very quiet, and just try to push all the thoughts out and ask for guidance. I'd do that for 15 minutes. I'd come back and I'd be rested. I'd feel great. I would have the answers and everything would really flow.

The thing is, when you're inspired in life—when you're truly inspired—everything else works: you feel better, the money seems to work, your relationships work, everything. "Inspired" comes from "in spirit." When you're in spirit, you're really following your bliss; you're really on purpose, and that's what you want to get to.

When you're in turmoil, you're not inspired; you're out of spirit, if you will—*dispirited.* So you want to get the spirit back. That's what the sacred self is.

Chris Mullin

Chris Mullin is a recovering alcoholic. He is a five-time All-Star for The Golden State Warriors and was chosen as a member of the Olympic Dream Team, featuring the NBA's finest. As a senior at St. John's, Mullin received the coveted John Wooden Award in 1985 and was named College Player of the Year.

The one part that was appealing to me was learning, not so much about myself, but about the disease. It just started opening up a whole new world for me. I still like to read about it; I like to read about other people. This is an amazing thing. If you don't know about it, you don't accept it. But when you study it and become educated on the disease, it all makes so much sense. It made it easier for me to quit.

When I was growing up, probably everyone I knew drank socially. Then again, a lot of people dominated their day with something that they couldn't wait to go and do, for whatever reason: sometimes because they were happy, sometimes because they were sad, sometimes just because that's what they did.

Since I grew up in that type of environment, I couldn't wait until I could go into the bar without hiding and sneaking. In a way, it was kind of getting my manhood. That's the way it was perceived: you get up there, and you can hang out with older guys and get accepted.

I drank a lot in college. We usually drank after every game. We were like the toast of the town, so we could go anywhere. If we won, we celebrated; if we lost, we'd drink and talk about somebody. My drinking really didn't affect me in college, and that's probably why it took a while for it to come to a head. I was doing as well as anyone in college. I was one of the best, so it did not become a focus. There were other things to distract me from what I was doing. When you're successful, other things are overlooked. When you're doing okay, you just leave it alone. If you're not doing well, you can find excuses.

Basketball-wise I was fine, although I could have been better in college. But socially I was hiding a little bit because I was pretty exposed, being in New York, being on a really good team, being one of the better players. Drinking was the way I was able to deal with that. Even to this day, some people would love the limelight, the publicity and the spotlight. If I could change one thing, I'd like to play in an empty gym and not be covered. A lot of this stuff comes to light later on.

Drinking helped me not deal with things, not deal with the spotlight. That's the way you deal with it, but in reality you're not dealing with it. If there was a party after the game in college at a frat house or one of the local bars, I preferred to go somewhere myself or with one other person that I felt comfortable with, have a few beers and then go deal with whatever was going on at the party. That was my routine. So when something came up, I was numb to it and everything was all right. Let's make it all right before I get there because it might not be all right.

The general manager of the Warriors, Don Nelson, approached me, saying that he wanted me in better physical shape. He really didn't come on that strong. He said, "You know, if there is a problem, we're more than willing to help; and if there's not, then you should be able to stop." I said, "Sure, no problem." Then that weekend, true to form, I was out drinking again, not really thinking much of it.

I came back my third season and struggled through training camp. I was out of shape. I dedicated myself to getting in shape enough to stay out of the doghouse, kind of tiptoeing that line. Then I started missing a practice or coming late, and that's when he confronted me and said, "There *is* a problem." He suspended me for a game.

I went home and my agent happened to be in town visiting a friend of his. We sat down and talked about checking into a treatment center. It was something I really didn't want to do at the time because, as you know, you don't really feel like giving it up—maybe for a few days, but not forever. I knew it would be highly publicized, but it's something I decided to *try* more than decided to *do*. I said, "You know what? I'm very unhappy. I'm not doing as well as I would like. Let's try it. Let's give it a month or so, and we'll see what happens." If something works, I'll go after it 100 percent. I'm that type of person.

The first two weeks I was very reluctant. I struggled and struggled with acceptance, but once I got over that part, I started learning. The one part that was appealing to me was learning, not so much about myself, but about the disease. It just started opening up a whole new world for me. I still like to read about it; I like to read about other people. This is an amazing thing. If you don't know about it, you don't accept it. But when you study it and become educated on the disease, it all makes so much sense. It made it easier for me to quit. I realized that I didn't have to take it all on myself that I fucked up or that I was this weird person.

Sometimes we get labeled, which is okay, but when you have the education and the understanding, it's a lot easier to sort that part of it out. Even now I hear comments during games. They don't say as much now, but earlier on when I first came back, they did. If I was having a bad game they might shout, "You're drunk!" or this or that. I look at them, and I pity them. I tell myself they just don't understand. I remember one time—I think we were in Phoenix— a guy was really getting on me. I didn't even cross words because he had a kid sitting next to him. I hope when his son grows up, this is not something that he has to deal with because someone his son meets along the way is going to need a little help. It might not be drinking; it might be something else. It's just that they're uneducated.

Now I can sit back and almost laugh at them, and again I pity them because society is so full of everything. Everyone has something to deal with. I really believe that every person in this world has some problem. It's not a bad thing to ask for help. Once you get it, it's the greatest thing. In a way, I felt relieved from all the pressure. I was trying to be a perfect player, perfect in public life, perfect with my family, and it was just too much. It was like bursting a pimple: you just let the pressure out.

Even to this day, when things come up, the first thing I do is get on the phone or go to a meeting, whatever my schedule is. I take care of it. When it's done, I feel so much better. Sometimes you think, "I know what they're going to say. I know what's going to happen." But every time you get there, someone says something, and it grips you.

I've been able to help friends and relatives, and that's rewarding, too. I would never have thought when I was 23 or 24 that at 32 someone else would be calling me and saying, "Hey, what do you think about this?" and that I'd be sitting down and chatting with whoever it may be. It comes full circle. It also helps me deal with so many other things.

Basketball is still very important to me, but I deal with it so much better than I did in the past. It used to be do or die. If we lost, I was a basket case; if we won, I was the happiest guy in the world. It's not like that anymore. As a professional athlete, if you let that dictate the way you're going to live your life, it's dangerous. No matter how good you are and how much you practice, you're going to have good and bad games—that's guaranteed. For that to be your barometer is dangerous, and realizing that helped me get a little more consistency and stability in my life.

I remember when my father used to come out to California and visit during my first couple of years with the Warriors, he'd bring the dog out with him from New York. I was always out running, coming in late, and he'd say, "Why don't you just sit down and pet the dog?" I'm like, "What's that?" Now I have two dogs of my own and, ironically, that's one of the best parts of my life. I go out in the backyard, sit in the hot tub, and these two dogs sit next to me outside the tub. I pet the dogs, and that's what I look forward to. When I was 23, I thought my dad was nuts. Like, to heck with petting the dog—I've got things to do! And now I'm going home to do that.

It was the same way with staying in shape. I'd do my best during the season, then in the off-season completely collapse. Now I work out continuously throughout the year. That positive reinforcement thing plays a lot with me. Like I said, when I first started out, sobriety was something that I was going to try, and it worked. I got into it more, and everything fell into place. Now the training is just a product of that. I worked out one summer—boom—it worked great. I had a great season, so next time I did it even more, and so on. I even carried it through when I was injured.

Going through therapy and rehab and having this serenity has helped me deal with that; it puts things in place. It makes me realize that it's not the end of the world. I've been away before. I've taken a month off before and come back. I've done it before, and I'll do it again.

The thing that I think sticks out most in my sobriety is that I was able to deal with my parents' death. If I had been out, I don't think I would've ever been able to deal with that. It was the toughest thing I ever had to deal with. I don't know what I would have done if I was in the condition I was in when I was 23 or 24. Being able to go through that sober—being able to cry, to feel the hurt and the hate with my parents dying three years apart—was the only thing that pulled me through. After that, I feel I can deal with anything.

Those were the two most crushing blows to me, but I think it was also a blessing. The timing worked out. Because I was sober I was able to help out my brothers and sisters. I think that in the past, I wouldn't have been there emotionally. I was able to take care of a lot of things that my younger brother wasn't able to take care of. I was able to be there for him like my parents had been there for me.

In the past, no one would have ever suggested calling Chris. Now my sister will call and say, "Hey, this guy is having some problems. Why don't you give him a call? He needs to talk to you." It's a total turnaround, and I'm proud of it. But that's what happens in time. They'll say, "Hey, call Chris. He's been through that. Give him a call and ask him how he handled it." It helps me also because, again, it's positive reinforcement.

A lot of times in sports you can play a great game. Someone will say, "Chris Mullin, the ex-alcoholic, had 30 points." It stays with you. But what you really need to focus on, and what's really important, is the way you can relate to people in everyday life. When I'm away from basketball, people approach me on a totally different level, on a human level—not "How do you shoot your jump shots?" When they say things like, "When your mom died, how in the hell did you get through it?" I do my best to give them some advice. Whatever it may be, there is a way to deal with it. There's definitely a way *not* to deal with it, and that's to drown yourself and not to laugh, not to cry.

I'll tell you what's interesting, what really makes me appreciate my recovery. It's my kids. Every day it's a test of being honest. The kids are asking you, looking you dead in the eyes and asking, "Where are you going? When are you coming home?" Those could be major questions when you're out there drinking. That could be two major blows. That's probably two I-don't-knows! Now I say, "I'm going to practice. I'll be home at 2:30."

I wouldn't have had any of these rewards if I didn't take that first step and look into straightening up. I was successful during my last year of college and the first couple years in the pros, but I was unhappy. There's a fine line because some kids drink, and it doesn't affect them. I think it's emotional: I was unhappy. I wasn't enjoying something that I loved to do because of alcohol. If you find yourself not spending time with your family, with people you love, if you find yourself not doing the things you like to do, there's a reason for it and you have to at least look into it. Give it a shot! That's the first step. That was my approach, and I ended up saying, "Wow, this is me!" Part of me said I didn't want it to be me. But there was no lying—it fit me like a glove.

Joey Ramone

Joey Ramone is the lead singer of The Ramones, one of the original punk bands to emerge from New York in the mid-1970s. They've had a ton of hits, including *Sheena Is a Punk Rocker, I Wanna Be Sedated, Rock 'n' Roll Radio, Blitzkrieg Bop, Gimme Gimme Shock Treatment, Howling at the Moon* and *Rockaway Beach.*

It really isn't enough just to be sober. It's like, what are you going to do with it now that you're that way? I saw that a lot of my friends were into different things: things that were nondestructive, and things that would make a difference, not just something that you talk about at a party and then never happens.

did a lot of hanging out, doing the whole thing—going to parties, talking to people, drinking. You know how it is. I'd hang out in after-hours clubs, going from party to party. It took a while to recuperate after partying that much. I woke up late, and it took some time for me to function. Partying really limits your ability to function.

I was getting pretty sick of my lifestyle and pretty sick of myself, sick of the kind of life that I was living. I started feeling a hollowness inside that felt really horrible. Then, ironically, I went to see a friend's band play at a club, and they invited me up for an encore. It was a place where I hadn't been, very dark with a high stage. When I was getting off the stage after the show, I was making my way down and twisted my ankle. I landed on my bone. I tore the ligaments real bad. The doctor said I'd have been better off if I'd have broken my ankle. It would have healed quicker. It was horrible, one of those real weird experiences. That night I was feeling great—I was on top of the world—and the next minute, I was fucked.

My ankle was so swollen that they put me in a temporary soft cast and told me not to put any weight on it at all. I was completely immobile for the next two weeks. I had to get a walker just to go to the bathroom. So I was just about bedridden and had a lot of time on my hands. After a couple days, I could hobble out to the living room. I was feeling good, considering that I was in a cast and had to postpone a tour and all that. I wasn't drinking because I wanted to heal faster. I was feeling inspired. I picked up my guitar and suddenly felt very inspired and started to write some really great songs, some that I hadn't quite finished because I hadn't been that inspired in a long time. It was exciting. There's a blockage when you drink a lot. It seems that my creativity just poured out when I was healing from my ankle. I was actually detoxing at the same time, and it felt good, real good.

There were times when I'd stop drinking for three weeks or so just to clean out. I was always very good about willpower, about being able to stop. I wouldn't say that I hit bottom when I messed up my ankle, or when I decided to stop drinking. There were a lot of things going on in my life that I wasn't that happy with. Drinking for me did have its high points, but for the most part I was getting kind of sick of my way of existence. So when I stopped drinking, it inspired me not to want to start again. I saw a drastic change in my thoughts, my feelings and my emotions. I've been excited about our band and excited about different projects we did, or certain albums, but this dose of inspiration was different, visibly different. It just felt too good to chance losing it by going back to drinking. I knew that once I felt it, I wouldn't want to lose it.

Things happen when you become sober. Things change. Your lifestyle changes, your friends change. I got a lot of new friends and they were really health-conscious—people who took care of themselves. Some were vegetarians, others were into macrobiotics and other interesting things. I've always been very adventurous about trying different things. So after getting sober for a while, I started working with a holistic chiropractor, which really opened me up and really got me into myself more. It really isn't enough just to be sober. It's like, what are you going to do with it now that you're that way? I saw that a lot of my friends were into different things: things that were nondestructive, and things that would make a difference, not just something that you talk about at a party and then never happens. These people were different. They were improving themselves, improving their minds. I wanted to try that.

It's great to be sober. I know that it's difficult for some people and somewhat easier for others. Everyone's different. Some people wrestle with it for years; other people find it. It's a wonderful feeling when you find it. You feel the results almost immediately. My mind was clear, focused. There wasn't any blockage. I never realized how much alcohol blocked all of the feelings, the emotions and creativity. You just get used to a certain lifestyle. I know *I* did. And for many years, I didn't think that the lifestyle I was living was that bad. I was successful, and I enjoyed myself. But when I messed up my ankle and faced a completely new set of events without notice, that's when I knew there was a different approach, that there was a different way to live. I was used to living the way I always did and never really knew of any other way to live. When some people discover sobriety, it's almost like a new high. I guess, for me, it was more that way.

Ozzy Osbourne

Ozzy Osbourne is a recovering alcoholic and drug addict. His previous works include *Diary of a Madman, Speak of the Devil* and *The Ultimate Sin.* He has had great success as leader of Black Sabbath, plus a solo career featuring 11 albums. His latest release, *Ozzmosis,* is the only work he has accomplished sober—and his most successful to date.

If someone said to me right now, "Ozzy Osbourne, there's a shot of booze here and I've got a gun to your head. If you don't drink that booze, I'm gonna blow your head off," I'd say to him, "Well, pull the fucking trigger," because there's no difference.

Let me tell you something about fear. The *Ozzmosis* record—I recorded it sober. I'd never recorded or written anything sober before. I thought if I didn't drink, I wouldn't be Ozzy anymore. It was a fear.

I started drinking because I lacked self-esteem. I was afraid, and it took away the fear. It gave me what we call "dodge courage." It allowed me to be outrageous. It broke the barriers, all my psychological barriers. I started off as this insecure kid, and when I took the booze it kind of masked over the insecurity. As my life went on, the insecurity came back, and I had not only an insecurity problem but an alcohol problem as well (plus anything else I was taking, which was just about anything).

I am not totally drug-free. I have to take Prozac; I have to take a thing called Celontin; I have to take a sleeping medication. But they are prescribed for a reason. I don't take a fucking handful of Quaaludes, down a shot of fucking white lightning and fucking go into town for three days. I do it under a doctor's supervision. I have to take the Prozac because I suffer from depression, which is a side effect from the years of alcohol abuse. I take the Celontin because I started having seizures. At the end of my drinking, I was in such a fucked-up state I came to a point where I had no choice. I had been in and out of treatment centers, to meetings. The funny side of it is that my wife and I decided that I should go to the Betty Ford Center, thinking they would teach me to drink properly. I had no idea what it was about. I thought I was drinking wrong and that they would teach me how to drink properly. I had been battling this because I knew I had a problem for a long time.

You ask people, "How do you describe denial?" Most people will say denial is when someone drinks or does something and denies that he has a problem. That is one form of denial. But denial comes in many ways, shapes and forms. To make me feel better, I would say, "Yeah, I'm an alcoholic, I fucking drink all day long. Now get me a fucking drink." I never thought I could function without it. I thought I wouldn't be able to write. I thought that people wouldn't want to know me. I thought, "What the fuck do you do? How do people survive without it?" I was in a haze all the time. The world was in a haze, and the only people that I would hang around with were other people that were in the same fucking bubble as me.

In my world, everyone was drunk. I would find bars where people drank more than me to make my conscience feel better. So if I would drink eight fucking pints of beer a day, I'd go to a pub where there were a lot of heavy drinkers so it wouldn't make me feel so bad. We alcoholics have incredible fucking tactical ways to us. I mean, if we could only put our brains to good use. The excuses! If I got up in the morning and it was raining, I'd say, "It's raining. I can't do anything; I'll go to the bar." If it was sunny: "Oh, it's a lovely sunny day! I'll have a drink." Any excuse, any reason: "I had a bad show last night—I'm gonna have a drink"; "I had a good show last night—I'm gonna have a drink"; "My wife is giving me a hard time—I'm gonna have a drink"; "We had a great time at the movies last night—let's celebrate and have a drink." Everything was around the drink. I would justify my drinking by attaching it to either a problem or something that wasn't a problem. I had to have a *reason* for drinking: "I'm on the road too long"; "I'm not on the road"; "My career's over"; "I'm successful"; "I have a number one album"; whatever.

So I tried to get off, and I tried therapy. I went to two treatment centers. Eventually—I can't tell you exactly when—I said, "It's over." I had to get outside help. I refused to go into another rehab. So what I did was get a live-in nurse who put me out for three weeks. I was on medication for three weeks—detoxing—and I was taken off slowly.

The desire to drink has left me. However, if I don't sleep, I have a sleeping pill. If I fuck up my back like I did the other day, I take a pain pill. It's for a different reason now. I know people who don't drink, and they don't have a numbing shot when they have their teeth drilled. I'm not that fucking out there. I do things for a different reason.

This is a milestone in my life. Honest to God, I never thought it was physically possible for Ozzy Osbourne to have fun, to enjoy life, to create without drinking. Now this is proof of what I am saying: I not only recorded the *Ozzmosis* album sober, I wrote it sober. My album entered the *Billboard* charts at number four. I never had such a high figure.

All these fucking years I was going around saying, "Man, I won't be Ozzy, I won't be a wild man, I won't make music if I stop drinking." I'd never done it before. I said to my therapist one day, "I feel like a bit of a fucking dick, sitting in a bar drinking Perrier water." He said to me, "Why do you have to sit in a bar?" I didn't even think of that. My life was bar, bed, bar, bed, hangover. In the old days I'd feel so dreadful from the night before that I would be longing for the last number so I could get off the stage and drink my bottle of fucking cognac. It was my treat after the gig. It just became very ugly.

If someone said to me right now, "Ozzy Osbourne, there's a shot of booze here, and I've got a gun to your head. If you don't drink that booze, I'm gonna blow your head off," I'd say to him, "Well, pull the fucking trigger," because there's no difference.

Every day I fuck up somewhere, and that's okay now. I'm bagging on myself for smoking these fucking cigarettes. I'm bagging on myself because I take these fucking medications all the time. But I'm aware now. I'm aware of my behavior. My behavior was unacceptable; I was out of control.

I didn't realize how many other people loved me—not just my immediate family, but the people who work for me, my audience. I was affecting everybody. It's a very selfish problem. What I'm saying here is you have to really be honest and soul-searching. You have to look yourself in the mirror. If you honestly enjoy waking up in your own urine and puke in some strange fucking place, not even knowing how you got there, then that's your problem. All I can say is I have a bed, and I know where I am. I don't wake up with a hangover. I am no fucking angel. I am not going to say to the world that I don't even take a fucking aspirin because that's bullshit. If I have a headache, I'll take an aspirin. If I can't sleep, I'll take a sleeping pill. But I do it for a reason. I am not out of control with it.

The desire to drink has left me, but I do have fun. There's proof to what I'm saying—just look at *Ozzmosis*. If someone said to me six years ago that I'd have the biggest album of my fucking career once I turned sober, I would never have believed them. I would have thought, "It's over. It's fucking over." I had one of my band members in here the other night. He drinks, and it didn't bother me. He said to me, "Man, my friend just got fucked up on a bike. I'm never going to ride a motorcycle again." Literally five minutes later he said, "Man, I'm never going to ride a motorcycle again." I said, "You already fucking told me." And I'm going, "This guy's having fun? He sounds like a fucking moron!"

Alcohol was my number one choice. After that, any shit would go down, anything. I'd go for the booze, then it would all fall in. I would wake up in the middle of the night to drink, then go to bed. I would get up in the morning and drink—all day, every day.

I don't want to come across as having a fucking halo above my head, but all I'm saying to you is drinking is no longer a problem. Because I don't drink I don't go looking for drug dealers. I don't do all that shit anymore. There's nothing on this fucking earth that would make me want to drink again. I know what would happen. It's just like what someone said to me, and it's the simplest equation: you have a room with two doors. The stupid thing is that when you're an alcoholic, you open the door where there's a guy standing with a baseball bat who whacks you in the head. When you come around, you keep going through the same door and keep getting whacked on the head. Then one day you go, "I wonder what the other door is?" You open the other door, and you don't get a whack on the head. Then you go, "Why didn't I do that before?" That's the way I looked at it.

I still have voices in my head all the time. I have a head full of fucking demons. I have a head full of bad people. The voices are there, and the only way that I can get satisfaction is if I don't act on what they say. I have a whole fucking planet of different little meanies in my head that try to fuck me up all the time. It sounds like I'm a fucking psycho or something. In the old days, this one fucking thing in my head would go, "Go on, take that fucking drink. You know you want to drink." So I'd take a drink. The next morning, the very same fucking voice would say, "See Ozzy, you can't fucking do it! What the fuck are you doing?" and it would drive me crazy, the same fucking voice. I've got lots of different things in my head, lots of different voices that would talk to me. I've got a haunted fucking head. My head tried to sabotage me all the time, but I've had a big argument with the fucking men in my head. I've noticed a few fucking things try to get me to drink, but it doesn't work. I have won that battle, and I know it.

I just don't drink anymore. It's not an issue. I don't get up and say, "Fucking day 93, 94, . . ." I just get up. It's kind of a weird angle that I look at it from. If I had my right leg amputated from the knee, I would have to accept the fact that I've only got one leg, right? I don't want to sit in a room for the rest of my life talking to other guys with one leg about how I lost my leg. I just have to accept the fact and get on with my life.

The old Ozzy I don't even know. If I was an animal, someone would have shot me in the head and put me out of my misery. I was just a very sad, pathetic individual. Bloated. Every night I would wet the bed. Every day I would throw up. Every fucking night I would do something stupid. I look at old photographs and I feel better at 46, and look better at 46, than I did when I was fucking 26. I work out now. I keep fit. I have a great relationship with my wife and kids. I have a great relationship with my peers and friends. Sure, I have bad days, but that's life. Some days the gig goes wrong, but there's nothing that a drink will do better.

Just say, for instance, that my wife phones up and says, "I've got another man. I'm going to leave you." I go to the show tonight, and the gig falls to pieces. I phone up my mom, and she dies—whatever. Whatever fucking reason you can think of. I know that if I was to pick up a drink, all of that would be there, plus I would be drunk as well. It would not have taken away the problem. The problem would still be there. All I would be doing is adding another problem to all the other problems by drinking because I can't fucking drink.

I never went out for a drink in my life; I went out to get fucked up on a daily basis. I said to my assistant Tony one day, "Do you want to come out for a drink?" He goes, "Okay." So we drive a distance to this bar. I get out and he parks the car. I go in the bar, get a drink and get him a drink. I drink my drink; he drinks his drink. I go, "What do you want now?" He goes, "Nothing." So I go, "What do you fucking mean, nothing?" He goes, "I don't want any more." I go, "Are you joking now? I thought you were coming out for a drink." He says, "I have. I've had a drink, and I don't want any more." I couldn't fucking understand that. I thought, "What the fuck are you doing, man? We drove fucking 15 miles to this bar, and you don't want any more." He says, "Ozzy, you didn't say to me, 'Let's go out and get fucked up,' because if you would have said that I wouldn't have come. You said to me, 'Let's go out for a drink.' I fancied a drink. I had a drink and that's all I want." I couldn't relate because I never went out for a drink in my fucking life.

Alcoholism is such a fucking selfish thing because you don't realize how you hurt people and how you react to things. It was the day after my daughter's birthday party. We had it at the house. My wife said to me, "You should have seen the state of you yesterday." I'm thinking back, and I'm thinking, "It wasn't that bad—I just had a few drinks." She kept going on, and she said, "Are you sure?" And I said, "Knock it off. Forget about it." And she said, "Do you want to see something?" I said, "What are you fucking talking about?" She videoed me. I put the fucking video on, and I could not fucking believe what an ass I was. I was doing running headbutts at the fucking door at my child's fucking birthday party. And I must have been in a blackout because I have no recollection of it.

The blackout thing scared me to fucking death. At times during binges, I would just disappear. I woke up in a different town. I didn't know where the fuck I was. I became a chronic blackout drinker. I woke up one morning in fucking jail in my hometown, charged with attempted murder. Apparently I attacked my wife and tried to strangle her. The police came in and actually charged me with attempted murder, but my wife dropped the charges. I went to court and everything, and I have zero recollection of it. What always frightened me was that some good person would someday say, "That's the man that ran my brother over," or "That's the man that put a fucking axe through my son's head." That's frightening.

I take a look at my old album covers and kids come up to me in stores with old photographs. You can look at the old photographs of me, look at my eyes, and see sadness. *I* can see sadness; I can see a sad guy. It's a good reminder. People look at me in those photographs and say that I look insane. That's because I *was* insane. It's that simple. Somebody told me once, "Just because you're a crazy drunk doesn't mean to say that you ain't going to be crazy when you're fucking sober. You are what you are, with or without the booze." I mean, I am still as crazy as fucking anything. When I'm performing, I go fucking crazy.

I don't mind being around people who are fucked up because I go, "Fuck, am I a lucky son of a bitch! I used to be like that, and now it's not even an option." Now that I'm sober, I am there on time, and I am hardworking. I put 190 percent of my effort into it. I fulfill my commitment. I don't make an asshole of myself. I still make mistakes. I don't beat myself up. You know what? I like me now. You have to like yourself. I like me a lot.

If you're reading this and you're still drinking, don't give up! Listen, life's too short. If you want help, if you want to stop, you can't do it alone—go get help. I'm living fucking proof that there is life without a fucking bottle of booze. I am talking to you sober. I do not sound like I had a fucking drink or a fucking shot of heroin or anything. I did it for *my* reasons. I don't want to change the planet, but if by talking I can help some fucking poor guy get his head out of his ass, then I'm doing okay. Remember, there *is* life without booze.

Dennis Hopper

Dennis Hopper is a recovering alcoholic and drug addict. He's directed and acted in a number of successful motion pictures, including *Easy Rider, Blue Velvet, Hoosiers, Speed, Rebel Without a Cause, Giant, Waterworld* and many others.

People have said things to me that were really important through this recovery process: simple things, very simple. I remember when I first got sober. Someone wrote on a chalkboard, probably because of Easy Rider, *"Easy Does It . . . But Do It!"*

I had built in such a strong endorsement for drinking and using drugs because, after all, I was an artist and it was okay for artists to do that. All my heroes as painters, poets or actors were all alcoholics or drug addicts. So to me it was my right, my God-given right, to take and use drugs. It became my task. I had to do it or I would never achieve the things I wanted, so I thought.

That was all fine and good until I got sober and realized that my drinking and using behavior may have been acceptable to me in the past—like John Barrymore and Richard Burton and W.C. Fields—but it was not acceptable in the present. In the present, I look at people like Dustin Hoffman and Meryl Streep. They are people who don't make a lifestyle of drinking or using drugs. They're doing really fine work and they're doing really fine work with their senses. I had to get sober to really see that. I think that when you start dealing with the arts and people in the arts, it's beyond denial: many people think it's their right. They have to go and seek the bottle. They have to seek the drugs and seek disorienting themselves. That's a tragedy in itself. I think that's a special problem.

The working man and woman are a different deal because they have the guilt right away that they shouldn't be drinking, that they shouldn't be out of control. At a certain age—once they go through their mating period and finding their manliness and getting into enough bar fights—there's a point that they have to grow up. At that point, I think they get into trouble: they get into denial.

I thank God that I got sober because if I hadn't, I guarantee you I would either be incarcerated or dead. I would not be talking to you now.

People have said things to me that were really important through this recovery process: simple things, very simple. I remember when I first got sober. Someone wrote on a chalkboard, probably because of *Easy Rider,* "Easy Does It . . . but Do It!" I think really the most important thing that anybody ever said is, "You just don't drink and you don't do drugs today." It's really that simple. Obviously it can become complicated, but think about it: you just don't drink and you just don't do drugs today. When you look at it that way, it's much easier to comprehend than the thought of not drinking for the rest of your life.

That pretty much gets you through it. It will get you through it because every day you do it, you don't drink. Pretty soon you come out of the fog. You come out of the dependency. You come out of the stupidity of, "I have to have it," "I must have a drink," "I must have some drugs." Once you get out of the "gotta have it" syndrome, your brain starts clearing. You start looking around and seeing things again and realizing who you are and where you are and what you want and what your dreams really are.

You can only do that sober. You can't really do that any other way, not if you're an alcoholic and a drug addict, because there's only a moment when drinking and taking drugs work. After that you're working for the drink and drugs, they're not working for you. I'm talking as a creator. Then pretty soon, if you're really involved in drugs and alcohol, you don't have your senses at all. You don't have any sensibility of your own. You become a schizophrenic, you become more and more paranoid—which you probably were anyway—until you lose sight of yourself.

So the mere fact of just stopping—not drinking and not doing drugs today, and being able to maintain that—causes the rest of the miracles to open up because you start becoming normal again. Your senses quiet down, and your vulnerability, your patience and your understanding start coming back. Certainly the 12-Step programs are the most important things that I've found anywhere. They really work. Those programs are there for everybody.

I had a manager who thought the way to handle me was to cut me off booze entirely. He told everyone not to give me anything to drink. It's a great idea. However, if you cut off someone who is drinking as much as I was drinking, there are going to be problems. I was drinking a half gallon of rum with a fifth on the side and several beers every day. If you take that amount of alcohol away from somebody immediately, his whole system shorts out. He starts seeing things, hearing things that aren't there and having total hallucinations. They used to call them d.t.'s. I went into these incredible hallucinations. I thought I was a hologram and I thought that World War III had begun—incredible stuff.

I was shooting a film in Mexico and got into a lot of trouble. Paranoia was really setting in. The police arrested me. A film crew came and rescued me, and they put me on a plane they had chartered to Los Angeles. On the plane I was hallucinating, and I crawled out on the wing in midair. I decided that Francis Ford Coppola was on the plane filming me. I had seen him, I had seen the cameras, so I knew that they were there. The crew started the wing on fire so I crawled out on it knowing that they were filming me. All this was a total hallucination, except climbing out on the wing, of course, which didn't last very long. I was out there and a bunch of stunt men grabbed me and pulled me in.

I had it a lot rougher than most people. I knew that I couldn't go back to using because I would be incarcerated. I went into a treatment center. The doctors put me in a medical unit and gave me a drug called Prolixin. It is an antipsychotic drug, but 7 percent of the population are allergic to it and it gives them Parkinson's disease. I had a psychotic reaction and it gave me Parkinson's disease temporarily.

When the doctors saw that happening, they gave me another drug called Cogentin to take away the Parkinson's. It didn't. It caught me between Parkinson's and whatever. I couldn't make sentences. I couldn't make gestures. I had Parkinson's and I didn't know what else I had. The doctors were taking me from meeting to meeting saying, "Look, this is what happens to you when you drink and use drugs. Here's a living example." I mean I couldn't turn my head. I couldn't make sentences. I couldn't get the cigarette to my mouth. It would take me five minutes to get my hand to my mouth, or to get the cigarette out of my mouth. Unbelievable.

When they finally released me from treatment, I was going back to Taos, Mexico, to kill myself because I was never going to be able to act again. I flew to Las Vegas and told this girlfriend of mine what I was going to do. The treatment program did not allow me to see my personal physician, so she got me on an airplane and flew me back to Los Angeles to see him. He examined me and said, "My God, they didn't give you enough Cogentin." He gave me a bunch of shots of this stuff, and finally he said, "That ought to do it." I got up and I put my hand in my back pocket. I made gestures. I made a sentence: I said, "My God, I'm back."

So mine was a different kind of recovery. When I got back to what I considered some sort of normal after spending four months being in this other hell, there was no way I was going to go out and do any drugs or have a drink. I had a really hard time during that episode, but it made it a lot easier to stay away from the booze and drugs. I didn't have any inclination to say, "Boy, I'll go to a bar and have a drink now. Wouldn't it be great to have a drink?" or "Wouldn't it be great to have some drugs?" I said, "Thank God I'm back. Thank God it's over." So it was a sort of erase and rewind. The experience had really humbled me, and I had gotten the message.

I was very afraid that I wouldn't be able to do things without alcohol and drugs, but, man, I can do it so much better. My work is so much cleaner. I can utilize all of my senses. Everything is clear now.

I never thought that was possible without drugs and alcohol because, again, I was an artist and that's what artists do. Then you look at the working man, and he looks at his buddies or his coworkers and thinks the same thing: that's what they all do so he doesn't have the problem. It's very acceptable behavior.

I was in Ireland for 17 weeks doing a film. I love Ireland and I love the Irish people, but they've based their whole society on drinking. They do what they call pub crawls. The women have pub crawls where they go out and go from one pub, and they crawl to the next pub. Their whole society is built on that. It's amazing. It's their way of life. But there are meetings there; there are people who are sober. There are people who don't drink, but the majority of people do drink.

Until you try the other side, you have no idea what you're missing. I didn't. I drank in front of everybody. I did drugs in front of everybody. I just assumed that everybody in the world was doing drugs and drinking. They certainly were around me.

As far as my family and the life that I had, that wasn't why I was drinking. No one was hiring me. I wasn't getting work. I was wondering why people were calling me difficult, but that's not why I was drinking. I was drinking because I was an alcoholic. I started as a kid, you know, hanging out with the guys. In Kansas, we used to go out in the pickup truck and get a bunch of beer. We would all make a circle with the trucks in the middle of a vacant lot or a field, and drink beer. When I was a kid, I worked on the harvest and the farmers used to give us beer because the sun was so hot. They'd feed us salt and the beer to cut the wheat.

When I was 18 years old, my agent gave me a martini. He said, "This is a martini, extra dry." I went, "God, this is awful," and he said, "It's an acquired taste." Boy I acquired that taste real quickly.

Drinking and drugs change everybody's behavior. They make people unreasonable. Not that we actors are necessarily reasonable people to begin with, since we work with our imaginations and our senses, but people do get out of control. I don't really see it anymore because I have a history and they know the history; it's a different kind of thing. The other actors check and balance themselves. They still drink in front of me and do all that, but I haven't had a problem with actors getting out of control. In fact, many of the people that I work with are the bad boys and bad girls, so to speak, in the business. They don't give me a problem. I don't preach to them and try to stop them from doing what they're doing because I think that's very bad for the program, for my program. I can't go out and try to convert this world, the people who are drinking and taking drugs, and try to convince them that I have the only way. That's just not my task in life.

These people don't want to get sober. At this point, I'm not about to try to convince them to get sober because it's a losing battle. Something somewhere has to humble them enough or hit them on the head like a sledgehammer so they understand that they *have* to get sober. That's something you can't give somebody. That's something he has to get by himself, or by some power beyond him or in him—whatever—that leads him to the conclusion that he has to get sober. At that point, then I can be helpful. Then he comes and asks for help, which is something that I look forward to, something that gives me great pleasure. You have to be there for people. You need to support people.

Serenity is a personal thing and it's different with everybody. You talk about quiet times like taking the time to smell the flowers, taking time to look at the flowers. I notice everybody is speedwalking, they're all speedwalking, they've all got somewhere to go and they have to go there quickly. They're not really looking around. They don't know where they are, they don't know what's going on around them, they just move ambitiously onto the next thing. The next thing will keep them going and driving for that. They're like horses with blinders on: they don't really see their life, they don't see where they live, they don't see what's around them, they don't have any connection with the real feelings of their time or society or family or work. Serenity is taking the time to pause, to meditate and to make a personal check on yourself. You'll just have a much fuller life and your life will be more complete. You might even have a little more understanding of things. Then there's always the possibility that you might become scared again because we live in a miracle. We are a miracle. This whole life and this whole complex society that we live in are very humbling. There's so much here to take care of and so much here to do that one needs serenity to keep a balance.

Chapter XI

FINAL THOUGHTS

These are better days.
Better days are shining through.

—Bruce Springsteen
"Better Days"

Sharing and Other Positive Solutions

Remember the facts: a moderate drinker and smoker is 15 times more likely to develop cancer of the throat, larynx, pharynx and esophagus than nonsmokers and nondrinkers. Recent studies have discovered heavy drinkers increase liver cancer risk by 400 percent. Combine drinking with smoking, and the risk escalates to 1400 percent. Alcohol is involved in 80 percent of fire deaths, 80 percent of snowmobile accidents, 77 percent of falls, 65 percent of drownings, 65 percent of murders, 60 percent of child abuse cases, 55 percent of arrests and 35 percent of rapes. More than 11 million American families have seen a family member killed or seriously injured by a drunk driver in the last nine years. Society's loss in wages, productivity, medical and legal costs caused by death and injuries in drunk-driving crashes exceeds $24 billion each year.

Enough of the stats: just look at what alcohol does to people's thinking. How many times have you made an excuse or a lie to go out drinking and using? Or maybe you were on the receiving end of the deceit. Many teenage pregnancies are caused when both parties have been drinking. What's the easiest way to loosen up a date? Give her a drink. It's worked for years. There are advertisements for malt liquor showing a man and a woman out on a date with the slogan, "It works!"

The fact is, alcohol is used to comfort many souls, to ease the pain, to relinquish the nervousness. What these practicing alcoholics don't realize is that once you're sober and stick to a program, the nervousness

219

fades, the fear transforms into faith and your soul becomes sacred. Here are a few final thoughts from many of the guests.

Nils Lofgren

The first year I found I was hanging on for dear life being clean and sober. That meant everything to me. I was on the road almost the whole time my first year, but all I did was stay clean and sober and I did my job. I was like an infant in this whole thing called recovery. The second year I started to want more than just to be able to say, "It's midnight and I'm straight."

I started liking myself instead of hating myself, instead of worrying about succeeding. All the crap about status and *he's got more than me* faded. I'd just go to the park and play some basketball for a few hours because that made me feel good.

The first year I was on tour and I never went to meetings because my attitude was, *Well, I'm on tour and I can't get to a meeting. I'm staying clean and sober.* I was able to do that because that's all I wanted to do. But the second year, I started to find meetings. What happened was, after the first year, I healed enough to start wanting genuinely not to just eliminate drugs and alcohol from my life, but to feel better, too. I didn't get clean and sober just to tell you I don't drink anymore; I wanted to feel better about myself. For a year that happened just by staying clean and sober.

After that, I started liking myself enough so that sobriety in itself wasn't enough. To heal further it was necessary for me to seek out meetings, to take some more of an active part in it. I know everyone has a different timetable with it, but that's how it went for me. In the third year, the road got narrower. It's like the more I heal, the more I like myself and the less I'm able to just sit around and be content just not drinking.

Doug Fieger

Somebody once told me that pain is caused by the effort it takes to hold onto an old idea. It's not caused by the new idea, it's caused by the effort it takes to hold onto the old one. Now, there are a lot of things to keep in mind when we get sober, a lot of slogans: *Easy Does It, First Things First, Let Go and Let God.* There's a lot of stuff to think about, but what else do I have to do? It's a hell of a lot better than thinking about, *Where am I going to cop next? My dealer's out of town.*

Tony Sales

It's not my parents' fault that I took drugs and alcohol or that I'm an alcoholic. It's actually no one's fault. It's not my fault, either. It happens. I might have acquired it along the way. I might have been born with it. It doesn't really matter. What matters today for me is that I live in the day, that I try to have a good time with my life because this is not a run-through for me, this is it.

Stevie Ray Vaughan

I kind of end up doing a little 12-Stepping in "Life Without You" every night. You'd be surprised how many people come up and say, "I got sober because I heard you say that." I'm just glad I'm able to do that, that I was put in a position to do that because I used to be in the position to crash and burn and have kids think that was cool. That's bullshit. It took me a long time to see that.

Steven Tyler

There's a five-day program at one of the treatment centers that deals with us being nothing more than a floppy disk—you and me—and we don't realize it, but the computer that we came out of left a lot of programming on our disks. Whatever negative points our parents had went on our disks as well as the positive ones. We don't know they're negative until we have them looked at and scrutinized.

Eddie Money

Things are much better, first of all because I don't wake up with a hangover anymore. I don't have to hide when I'm getting loaded. I don't have to look for that bundle; I don't have to look for those rolling papers. I don't have to make sure I've got a beer hidden under my seat. I can drive and say, "Hi," to a cop.

Cocaine and using drugs is a big lie. I don't have to lie to myself anymore. I can get on the phone and say to the office, "Hey, man, this is what I want and I'm not talking out of my asshole." I'm straight and I get a lot more respect.

God gave me a certain amount of talent. My mother says it's a gift I abuse. I think I should put this talent in the right direction. I don't want to see kids go out and get high, but then again it's not hip to tell kids not to get high.

John Ratzenberger

I was going into bars at 17 and 18. I couldn't drink, but I could get in. I used to listen to the older guys sitting at the bar—try it sometime. Go to a local bar and listen to the conversations and it's always, "You know, if I had only done that. If I had only bought that piece of land 15 years ago," or "Jesus, I should have taken that job with Amalgamated Aluminum Siding. I could have been manager today." It's always I coulda, I woulda, I shoulda. Even at that age I thought, *Well, why the hell didn't you,* and it took me a few years to realize they didn't because they were drunk all the time.

China Kantner

There are two guys I knew who were sober for a year or two and ended up going back out. One died of a heroin overdose. The other one was in his apartment and couldn't find any coke after calling some people. He freaked out and hung himself. That's even more devastating than people who don't enter recovery. That's one message I want to give to people, especially teenagers: how deadly this disease is. These two guys were very smart. They had used drugs a lot, they got into a program, spent a year or two getting fed this information at meetings all the time, and got help from people. They went out twice and they died. That's how devastating this disease is. People don't realize it. One of these guys was 19 and engaged to this girl, who came home and found him dead with a needle in his arm.

Gregory Harrison

By the time you realize you have a problem, it's an old problem.

Father Leo Booth

I find it less difficult to be honest than dishonest because being dishonest for me was rather painful. I've always believed that it's easier to be healthy than it is to be sick. That's a very important step because most people keep repeating and saying, "It's hard to get well, it's hard to recover, it's hard to get the program." And I think that as long as you give the emphasis to the fact that it is hard, it will remain so. But I actually think that it's easier to recover than it is to be a drinking alcoholic.

Nils Lofgren

I was going once a week to a psychiatrist just to deal with this problem, and I was lying to him. I was that sick—paying somebody for help and lying to him. I figured, *I can take care of myself and this way I can keep my life together.* Then the shit hit the fan.

Anthony Kiedis

I always liken it to Dr. Jekyll and Mr. Hyde because that's what I felt, especially on cocaine. I could be a fairly coherent human being one minute and ingest even the smallest amount of that particular drug and just turn into a raving, insidious, maniacal being who you really wouldn't recognize as being me if it weren't in this body. I mean, the length that drug addicts go to in order to get what they want when they either need it or when they're on it. If you could apply that type of intensity, that sort of devilishly creative and clever intensity toward a more positive goal, it's frightening what somebody could accomplish.

Steven Tyler

It's a miracle I'm here. I should be dead. There were enough toxins in me to kill ten people. There were these famous lost weekends. I'd go away on Friday and get totally wiped out. I didn't know who I was, how much coke I had snorted or what I was doing. I was the most obnoxious creep. People would always tell me what a jerk I was when I was high.

I have an addictive personality. I'm high-strung and impatient. I've got to have everything yesterday. I've got all this nervous energy that I've got to get rid of. Drugs and booze seemed to help me cope.

I grew up with the John Wayne mentality. If you were a two-fisted drinker, you were cool. I wanted to be cool. As a kid in the Bronx where I grew up, I was this goofy, white, big-lipped, jerky-looking kid. I wanted to be cool. Eventually I turned into a flaming alcoholic. In the 1970s it was cool to do drugs. If you could go to a party and have a girl on your arm and do all the drugs in the place, you were cool. I was cool—but I paid the price.

Dallas Taylor

Most of the kids I work with come from dysfunctional families. Most of their parents are alcoholics. There's a lot of physical, sexual, emotional and verbal abuse. You know, parents in the 1960s just didn't get it. There are the other extremes of abuses, too, like letting their kids do whatever they want. Well, kids need boundaries. It lets them know they're loved. You know, "I care about you. You can't do this, you can't do that." It's giving them the message that you love them. If you let them do whatever, then it gives them a message that you don't give a shit.

What is happening more and more is that families are recovering. It's not just the identified patient, it's not just the alcoholic kid, it's not just the acting-out kid. It's the entire family.

Everyone is sick in their own way. Even the kid who's an over-achiever is probably in just as life-threatening a situation as the kid who's drinking and getting F's. They're setting themselves up for a nervous breakdown or disappointment, a heart attack, workaholism, whatever. They're just acting out their own dysfunction.

Doug Fieger

By the time I had destroyed my career and my life started going down the tubes, there weren't many people around. The only people around were people who had a vested interest in me remaining that way because they were that way, too. Or they wanted the excitement of the kind of person who was an out-of-control, drunken, stoned maniac. That's the kind of person I was. That's the kind of people who hung around me. So by that time, by the time it was painfully obvious I had a problem, there weren't very many people around to point out to me that I had a problem. Up until that point, when people pointed out that I had a problem, I would always come back with, "But I'm very successful, so fuck you."

The reality is that I held my liquor and drugs really well. People who weren't close to me didn't know I had a problem.

In fact, when I got sober and made my amends to people in the business whom I'd done things to, they were astounded. They looked at me and said, "I never knew you drank," because I was the type of drunk who totally controlled my outward behavior. I was going crazy on the inside, but what people saw on the outside was very controlled.

But the people close to me—the band, my manager and my girlfriends—people around me saw a very strange individual. But I was the goose that laid the golden egg. It was my band. I'd written most of the songs, and it was my concept and my energy that sort of fueled the thing.

Lou Gossett Jr.

For anybody who thinks it's too late, if you're still breathing, you have a chance. And you can go further than your wildest imagination. You can get better than your wildest dreams. All you have to do is show up at the meetings. Show up, learn how to work the program, be of service and embrace the fellowship, and get on the train. You don't have to be the conductor; just be a passenger. It's okay to be the passenger.

Wayne Dyer

You need to ask yourself some questions: Are you at peace? Are you happy? Is your life working? Do you feel you are on a mission? Do you feel that you've discovered your life's purpose? And if the answer to any of those questions is *I'm not sure,* then you have to start consulting your higher self.

Dennis Hopper

It takes so much time to score and you spend so much time drinking in bars. You waste so much of your time. When I got sober, I felt that I had to make up for lost time. I couldn't believe where all this energy came from, where all of the drive came from. That's why I'm always working. I need to make up for lost time.

Steven Tyler

We had a visionquest of Aerosmith the other day, asking, "What are we going to be doing for the next decade?" We all went around the room and talked about ourselves. I was scared to death. I stood up. It's one of those things that I like to jump into. If something bugs me a little and I'm afraid of it, I have to jump in there and face it. You get right back on the horse after it throws you. That can be the most frightening thing to do; my heart was pounding out of my chest.

One of the easy things now is I immediately say, "I'm scared to death." I talk about what's going on in my mind. If you hold things in, you kind of internally hemorrhage, whereas if you get it out and talk about what you're feeling at the moment, it really breaks the ice.

Gregory Harrison

I look back now and see about an 8- or 9- or 10-year period of no growth as an actor, no growth as an artist. No risks, no stretching, no challenges—none of the things I'm feeling so good about doing today: experimenting and trying things. During that period, I spent so much time and energy recovering from and tending my addiction that I had very little energy left with which to grow as an artist or as a person. It's easier to measure your growth as an artist when you look back. I also know that as a person, not only did I not grow, I shrank.

Eventually, I shrank as an artist. That was probably one of the most horrifying aspects the month prior to entering rehab. Not only were all those other things wrong; I knew that I was no longer an actor I could respect. When your whole life has been devoted to that, that's a pretty shattering recognition.

I'm freed from the weight of addiction. I feel freed as an actor to take chances, to not fear falling on my face. Whatever humiliation might come from trying something that didn't pan out—the theater audience didn't laugh when they were supposed to, or they'd laugh when they weren't supposed to, or fellow actors tease me about it later, or a critic writes something bad about me, whatever—it's so lacking in potency compared with my priorities now. The humiliation turned into the good, honest humility of admitting my problem, my disease, going in and seeking treatment and humbling myself before a lot of people and before my higher power. It's like I don't have fear anymore; I have healthy caution. I try to make sure I understand the repercussions of making a bad choice, but the worst that can happen will not affect the fact that my daughter's going to love me when I walk in the door.

Now I'm living for the process of it. I'm much more likely to achieve more of the result because I no longer focus on the result. I focus on how much fun I'm having right now—today.

Earnie Larsen

There's love and there's love denied, and that's it. That's the way I want to open my next book: "There's love and there's love denied, there's nothing more."

Eddie Money

I was straight for about nine months, then I smoked a joint and went on stage and the band's going, "Oh God, don't tell me he's gonna get back out there again" because I turned Eddie Money into Eddie High. I did a show and I was loaded on pot and I thought I sang better, I thought my moods were better. I listened to the tape and I wasn't half as good, I wasn't half as sharp. But I was under the impression—being that I was stoned—that I thought I was better. It was a facade, it wasn't true.

The greatest thing about being straight—the most fabulous thing about being sober or not getting high—is you get used to it. Just like when you were a kid. I didn't get high when I was a kid. I have the same thing I had when I was a kid.

Dallas Taylor

One of the things I feared most was that I wouldn't be able to play if I gave up my cocaine and drugs. I wouldn't be able to create. I think you probably hear that a lot from musicians and actors: "God, I won't have that edge." For some reason we get into this illusion that we have to live this alcoholic, miserable, blues life in order to create. It's just bullshit. It kept me loaded for many years, just the fear of losing that ability.

What's it like now to play? I'm better than ever. My playing is better than ever. I'm more than I've ever been. At the peak of success with CSN&Y, very few people recognized me or gave a shit who I was, but today people know who I am and it's not just because of my drumming. I'll have a family come up to me and go, "God, man, did you do something great with my kid. You know, he's going to school and he's happy. Thank you for giving us our life back." To me that's every bit as good as, "Gee, can I have your autograph? I loved your last record."

John Ratzenberger

There are still residuals from living in the situation I was in. A lot of it, I figure, *Well, it's always going to be there. I just have to sit on it.* But the other stuff, you know, the child within . . . what I did was go to meetings and someone said, "Sit there and imagine yourself as a kid sitting on your own lap now. What do you want to tell this kid?" And that pretty much nailed me because I was a good kid. I just didn't deserve what happened to me.

Kids don't ask for this. Every now and then I just keep thinking of that situation of me as a kid, sitting on my own lap—the conversation—"How are you doing?" Thinking about whether the kid's proud of you or not, or whether you let that kid down. There's also the joys of having children now. I can do stuff I couldn't do as a kid. Not that I wasn't allowed to; I was scared to.

Anthony Kiedis

People are so afraid that the fun will go away. They have the attitude from looking at other people who have been high for so long, people like Jimmy Page and Keith Richards and whoever else has been doing it for all these years. These guys may be rock 'n' roll legends, but they are sad, miserable, bloated pigs when it comes right down to it. I don't mean to discredit their work or say that they're bad people, but I know a lot of people who come in contact with these guys and they're not happy people, they're really not.

I'm not going to sit here and talk shit about Keith Richards, but from what I know, the guy is just a walking zombie. I guess if that's what you want out of life, maybe you should follow in his footsteps. For me, being awake and alert and just invigorated by the fact that you're standing in a field of grass beneath a blue sky is a lot more special than being in a hotel room with a needle in your arm and not really tasting the fruits of life. I don't care if it sounds hokey because that's what I get off on.

I get off on scuba diving and the underwater world of space and sound and color and things like this, and that just doesn't happen when you're using drugs. At least it didn't for me.

Nils Lofgren

Alcohol and drugs worked for me. I thought they helped me enjoy life, helped me get through it. Somewhere in my mid-20s it all started turning on me and stopped working completely. Being high was my higher power, my best friend. I decided for 10 years after that that it's going to work tomorrow if it didn't work today; it was just a bad day. I was miserable, I was demoralized, but I'd wake up the next day and be hung over, thinking, *I'll never drink again,* and by the evening my body would recover and I'd be at it again, just desperate for it to work.

Grace Slick

Alcohol more or less dictates an entire lifestyle, so you aren't just taking away the alcohol, you're taking away a whole set of stuff that you like and is a part of your way of living. It isn't just taking away the alcohol, it's the whole attitude, the way of life. Sorry, that's gone. That whole deal's gone.

I didn't even talk to people who didn't use drugs. I just couldn't conceive of what they were doing. When I was in the band I didn't know anybody outside of the music business, nobody. The only people I talked to were doctors, when once every five years I'd go to the doctor. I have been relatively healthy up until about 48. Let's see, that's the doctor. Maybe you talk to somebody at Safeway when you buy something, a bottle of booze—you talk to the salesgirl. How long does that take? Three, four, maybe five seconds, something like that. I didn't know anybody who didn't use drugs except for Pete Sears who was our bass player, but he used to use drugs and stopped, had a spiritual experience. I really didn't hang out with Pete. I liked him fine. Oddly enough, he was the only one I didn't argue with.

Gregory Harrison

My only thought whenever anybody came to me for anything, whether it was for a part in a play or an autograph to sign, was, *How will this affect my ability to take my drugs?* Anything that would enhance it, I would do. Anything that would threaten it, I wouldn't do. *You need me to sit in a room without being able to leave that room for three hours? I'm sorry, I'm not available for that. You want me to leave the country, you want me to go to Java to film a movie? Don't they kill people if they have cocaine on them? I'm sorry, I don't like the script.*

Earnie Larsen

For me, God is spelled g-o-o-d. Picture the greatest good that you can think of, the deepest love, what is most precious to you. I often use my grandkids. Just focus on that sweetness and focus on that goodness and focus on that energy. Focus on what it feels like when someone you truly love just reaches over and takes your hand. That's God.

Do you have a God that is truly the embodiment of love, the deepest kind of love you can understand? That is helpful to me because most of us, when we think of God, think of God as an adult.

All of us have such scars relative to adult love and adult relationships. I have found my greatest image and my clearest avenue to God is not adult to adult, but adult to child. When I reflect how my grandkids are to me, then I know how God wants me to be with you.

Stevie Ray Vaughan

Here's an example of how powerful this disease is. I had to take a flight to get to the treatment center, so I borrowed $10 from my mother, told her I was going to buy some cigarettes, but instead I went straight to the bar and ordered double shots of Crown because I realized that I'd never flown on a plane before when I was sober. I had just left this clinic where they gave me all this information about what was wrong with me. I learned about the problem and how to deal with it, and I still fell right back into my old way of thinking. I still fell back into all those fears. Isn't that something? I thought, *Gee, I've never done this before,* and all the fears immediately took over and I still, after all the knowledge and information I received, I still resorted to my old ways of thinking. That's how strong this disease is. Your old habits will overpower you unless you train yourself with new ones.

Eddie Money

I don't even know what dry beer is. There's all these new beers out there; I don't even know what they are. But I'll tell you the truth: when I got high I used to love to get high. To me that was all part of the rock 'n' roll pattern—you know, chicks, all of that. The only reason I'm smoking cigarettes and doing this interview outside right now is because I quit smoking cigarettes for six months. When I went back to the studio, I started smoking again. I didn't start drinking, I didn't start snorting blow, I didn't start smoking pot, but I did start smoking cigarettes. And now my wife, now that she's seen the new me, she'd have a fit if she saw me smoke inside. I don't want to smoke in the house around the kids; smells up the house and, you see, once they get a whiff of what you could be, you can't go back.

Dallas Taylor

The most frightening thing that ever happened to me was when I realized I had to go the rest of my life without drugs and alcohol. That's when I really understood the reason behind one day at a time, one minute at a time sometimes, because that was a really frightening, overwhelming thought. I mean, drugs and alcohol were my best and only friend for many years, the only things that I could really truly depend on.

Father Leo Booth

Rarely is there any major violence, domestic or otherwise, that alcohol doesn't accompany.

Anthony Kiedis

I was never really fooled by the delusion. I always knew that I was incapable of creating great art under the influence, and it was always during minor spells of sobriety that I would get the brunt of my writing down. The funny thing is, the first two records came at a time when I wasn't thoroughly controlled by heroin. I was doing a lot of cocaine, a lot of speed and a lot of drinking and pot. Then we went through a terrible dry period, and right before we made *Fight Like the Brave,* our third record, I got clean for 50 days. That was the first spell, and I wrote that record in those 50 days when I was just totally amped on being alive and being clean. Then the day before we went into the studio, I went back out because once again I was facing the pressure of having to make a record. I was afraid and insecure. I thought I was going to do an inadequate job of performing for the record, so I went out and stayed up for a few days on drugs. Then I came back to the program, got clean, made the record, and on the last day I was so proud of myself for finishing it and doing what I thought was a great job that I went out and celebrated by doing a bunch of heroin.

Music is like the face of God. The only art that's really going to stand the test of time is the art that is born out of pure honesty, of your experience. Maybe you can have a drug-oriented experience and write about it later when you're not high and it's going to contain emotionally potent concepts because it's coming from a standpoint of honest experience, but I was never able to communicate it while I was under the influence, although I must admit I did write a few good songs on speed. I don't know why. This certainly isn't a promotion for that stuff because if you want to turn into a living cadaver, I recommend you take speed. That's what it did to me.

I never could perform properly on any drugs or any alcohol. The shows that I did under the influence of either heroin or cocaine were always a real letdown for me and probably for anybody who saw us. Fortunately, it was just one of those things that didn't happen as often as you might think. Somewhere deep inside I knew that was the one hour of the day that I had to have it together. After I was finished, I would go off and I'd wake up at five o'clock the next day and just try to get my head together for that show. It didn't really accelerate to the point of complete collapse until near the end of my using. Up until that point, I always managed to get off stuff long enough to go on tour, and then it all fell to pieces.

John Ratzenberger

The problem with education in America is that we're told we go to school to get an education so we can get a job to make money. That's what I was told and that's what most kids in America are told. That's not the point of education. The point of education is to learn how to learn, to learn how to deal with everyday events, to learn how to sift information and how to use it; but the end of that road is not to make money. If you get a job and do something that you love doing and you do it well, you're going to make money, that's a fact of life. You're going to make money because you do it well and you love what you're doing.

That's all it takes because eventually people are going to find out about you. But if you're in a job just to make money, you're never going to make enough money. The carrot is always going to be at the end of the stick and it's always going to be beyond your reach, no matter how much you make.

So you've got kids on street corners making $300 a day selling crack. Well, that's what they've been told all their lives: "You go to school so you can make money, get a job to make money." "Well, look how much money I'm making, Ma. I'm a success, right?" That's not it. That's just not it.

Steven Tyler

We had Guns N' Roses as our opening act on the *Permanent Vacation* tour. They were partying like we used to. Sometimes I wanted to strangle them because I could see what they were doing. But I can't say to those guys, "Don't get fucked up. Quit drinking your Jack Daniels."

Slash is shaking just like Joe Perry used to shake. But that's okay, he's going to learn for himself. I can only say, "This is what happened to me," and show them the scars.

Nils Lofgren

The hardest part for me in this whole process is to really heal and get well. You can't just stop drinking and using drugs. You have to heal as a human being spiritually. I can no longer sit on the fence. If I don't do some kind of healing on a regular basis, I backslide. It doesn't mean I have to use drugs, but I get miserable and that's a threatening thing. I think that's what keeps many people from getting help. It's about getting in touch with your feelings, starting to embrace who you are and all that goes on with that. This includes not only the good parts of you, but all the bad parts and facing up to it, wading through it and not running away from it anymore.

Wayne Dyer

People aren't used to meditating. Many people aren't comfortable with just quieting themselves.

So this constant chatter of our inner voices is what people consider to be normal. They don't realize that if you want to get to the higher place within yourself, you must be quiet and listen. The sacred part of you just wants you to be at peace. That's all it wants. If you ever have to ask yourself, "Is it my ego or is it my sacred self that's pushing me?" you should ask the question, "Does it bring me peace? Is this going to bring me peace?" And if it doesn't, then it's the ego, which is in a constant state of turmoil because it has you believing who you are is all you experience with your senses, that you have to prove yourself and you're in competition with others, and so on. I think of the ego as insane because it convinces you that you're something you're not. I mean, it would have you believe that you are only this body, and it denies the higher part of yourself.

Tony Sales

I was sober for a week or so, and I went into the den and realized that most of the books I had on the shelves were autobiographies of dead guys, entertainers that had snuffed themselves. I thought, *This is interesting. Why am I hanging around here?*

It was good that I became aware of that. I didn't want that. And even though my head had told me I wanted it, I took the alternate action. I wanted change so much I would do whatever it took. I still do whatever it takes to stay clean and sober. Staying clean and sober is the priority of my life because without it I have no life. I know that. I proved it to myself and I need not do that again.

Larry Gatlin

I felt like I had the flu all the time because I was either hung over or mad because I couldn't find any more dope. That paranoia sets in. Fear and anger are just extensions of the same thing. I was afraid all the time, so the only way to counteract that was to get mad. It was everybody else's fault that my life had turned into shambles.

Earnie Larsen

You're never going to stop drinking by willpower or any of that kind of stuff. You're never going to get rid of the issues by finesse, by ignoring them or by just trying to bulldoze them out of the way. That ain't the way it happens.

Dallas Taylor

I think passing on sobriety through living the example is a lot more effective than the preaching aspect. It's difficult, though, to not want to shout at the world because it's a great experience, especially when you're talking about someone who was hopeless and dying before they got sober, and then all of a sudden was full of life. Living the example is the best way of spreading the word.

Doug Fieger

The truth of the matter is, if you're going to get sober, you're not going to get struck sober—you're going to have to work for it. Everybody's got to work for it. It doesn't just come to you.

Eddie Money

I did a lot of crying, I was upset with myself. We were ready to have a baby. It was tough. It was horrible hitting rock bottom again. I was trying to kick the booze. I wasn't doing a lot of blow because I was making a record, but I was doing a lot of drinking, sneaking a lot of vodka. I started this record and the vocals weren't coming out right. Then someone turned me onto this Ecstasy, and I took those damn things and wound up with an ulcer. I couldn't get the stuff out of my system. It was in my system for about two months. I turned around in the studio and all of a sudden this Ecstasy would hit me again, and I hadn't done it for three weeks. It was horrible.

Nils Lofgren

Part of the problem with alcohol and drugs is that not everything I did sucked. If it had, I would have either had to quit or give up my whole life anyway. But that's part of the cunning, baffling, insidious thing about it: it allowed me to not only get more and more addicted, dependent, miserable and basically lose myself spiritually; but at the same time all that was occurring, it still didn't keep me from doing well enough on the outside and seeming okay to everybody.

Mike Binder

My father had a whiskey cabinet above the stereo in our living room filled with bottles of booze.

He was so afraid of drugs; he heard that there were a lot of kids on drugs and he used to say to us, "Don't get into drugs. There's a liquor cabinet full of stuff here. As long as you don't go anywhere, you can get drunk all you want." He was doing that as a deterrent. I would take a big bottle of Canadian Club and I'd go next door in an empty lot and I would just get drunk off my ass.

This was the sixth or seventh grade, and as soon as marijuana became fashionable, I immediately left the booze and got into marijuana. I actually went through a long period when I didn't drink, I just smoked dope. It was the same thing, it gave me the same inner glow, that same fuzziness. It stopped my brain from thinking, and what my brain was usually thinking was negative thoughts about who I was, what a loser I was.

You get into comedy as a *Hey look at me, hey love me,* and the reason you do that is because you don't think you're enough. The booze—and then later the pot, and then later the booze again—was something that would kind of quell that inner voice. It would quiet it down.

Years later when I got out to California and was a doorman at the Comedy Store, we used to do cocaine, which gave me the sense of importance. It kind of picked up my self-image a little bit, but the booze and the pot—all it did was quiet the negative thinking.

What I've learned over the years is that what you think you are is what you are. This is above and beyond recovery. If I think something can happen, that I can achieve something, it happens. If I think I'm capable of doing something, I'm capable of doing it. And if I think I'm not, if I think I'm a loser, I am a loser.

John Hiatt

Close to a year before I sobered up, I went to see my doctor for a physical and he said, "If you keep this up, you're probably not going to see 40." I was 32 at the time and, to show you where I was at, I thought that was a pretty good deal. That was my life. It wasn't about possibilities then; it was pretty much an open-and-shut case. So today I savor every minute. I would like to live as long as I can.

Anthony Kiedis

I went into a hospital with a lot of bruises on my arms. I wasn't really strung out because I'd only been doing it for a week or so. It was actually pretty easy to quit the last time because I didn't have the physical addiction. I had a monster of a mental addiction, but in the hospital I was not really forced; I was given the opportunity by the staff to learn how to face the fears and the pain and the sadness. I was able to go through them and to get to the other side, which is known as dealing with life on life's terms—something that I've always skated around. You'd be surprised how much easier it is to walk around without all of that inside of you, and also without the armor that we constantly wear. I just learned how to deal with it.

It was the greatest experience. Here were 20 patients in the hospital, ranging from the age of probably 65 to 11 years old. All these people knew that it was time to change their entire lives. The biggest change in their lives was already taking place, and for me it is still the single most essential experience of my life: going to that hospital because clean is the only way I want to live my life until the day I die. I know that it's something I do one day at a time because today all I have to worry about is not getting high today—you know, living my life as honestly as I can. I've pretty much lost my desire to use heroin or cocaine or alcohol or smoke pot or anything because I just like it so much sober that I can't imagine wanting to distort my perception. I've distorted it enough in the past to know what that's about.

I really don't know what it's like being this clean for this long, and the experience is far more exciting and far more rewarding, and I'm into it. I'm really into it right now.

Father Leo Booth

Spirituality is being a positive and creative human being. We don't have a message, we *are* the message. That's when a person has had a spiritual awakening. It's not what you say, it's who you are.

Steven Tyler

When I have cravings, I talk about it immediately with someone. I've found that I've tapped into this spirituality. I ask my higher power to take away the cravings. In fact, everything that I've asked my higher power since I've been straight, I've received.

Doug Fieger

The people who were my friends when I used, even in the late stages of my abuse, tried their best. But, you know, we alcoholics are people who are incapable of forming a true partnership with another human being. Consequently, we are these masks, dealing with other masks. The people we attract are people very much like ourselves. I had drinking buddies, I had using buddies, I had concubines, I had sex slaves, I had roadies, I had people who worked for me. I didn't have any friends. The people who were really my friends or wanted to be my friends, who were genuine, didn't want to be around me after a while, so they just disappeared.

Now I form relationships based on mutual respect, love, honesty and caring. I have more friends than I've ever had. You know, listening to myself talk I can imagine somebody outside listening to me and it all sounds so pat and so formula, so Pollyanna; and yet this is the truth, this is the honest-to-God, bottom-line truth. You see, sobriety is only as powerful as the effort you put into it. It isn't just not drinking or not using drugs. It's about confronting your imagined truths and bumping up against some real truth, and trying to put the two together with humility. That's what sobriety is for me: recognizing that there is a power greater than me in the universe. Call it what you will, there is a God and I'm not him. That's the reality of my life today. I never had that reality before, and I'm not a religious guy. I was raised by two radical atheists and yet I am profoundly conscious of a supreme order in the universe. I'm convinced that even though I may never know the purpose of this place, this vale of tears, I'm convinced that there must be a purpose. Part of how I can serve that purpose is by staying sober and telling people what it was that happened to me, no matter what it sounds like to them.

Chris Mullin

My mom and I always had a tight relationship. My father and I, we were tight, but it was up and down—a lot of mood swings and things like that. He got sober probably when I was in high school. He got his stuff together. I could tell something was happening because he became consistent, and his demeanor changed. He no longer had the mood swings. He didn't come home from work cranky. He was always the same, always happy, always where he said he was going to be. I mean, he was never bad, but I could sense a difference. The arguments around the house went away. We didn't know *why* right away, but we found out.

Ozzy Osbourne

I can honestly say to you right now that I don't miss it or want it anymore. If I did, I'd call room service, and I'd order a fucking crate of fucking booze. It's not an issue. I don't do it anymore.

It's not a race to see how many sober days I have because how many days *do* I have? I got today. I didn't drink yesterday. I may drink tomorrow; I don't know. I hope not. But I'm not going to drink today. I know *that* for a fact.

Joey Ramone

When I had my accident and stopped drinking, it was like a detox for me, just draining the alcohol out of my system and opening me up to a lot more. It's about feelings. I was feeling more in tune with myself, my feelings and my emotions. I was feeling things that I had never felt.

Whatever you may do when you're on alcohol or drugs, you're not in touch with yourself. With sobriety, I'm in touch with myself completely, and I like it much better that way.

Mike Binder

The life of drugs and alcohol is just a rotten trip. The journey into sobriety is a beautiful voyage: it gets better every single day. The more time you have away from drugs and alcohol, the better your life gets. And for someone reading this book who wants to get sober and wants to clean up their lives, and they're really serious about it, hold onto your ass because you're in for a great ride.

Chapter XII

AMAZING

I kept the right ones out
And let the wrong ones in;
Had an angel of mercy to see me
through all my sins.
There were times in my life
When I was goin' insane,
Tryin' to walk through the pain.

When I lost my grip
And I hit the floor,
I thought I could leave
but couldn't get out the door.
I was so sick and tired
Of livin' a lie,
I was wishin' that I would die.

—Steven Tyler
"Amazing"

*F*ive days before my deadline to hand in this book, I moved into a hotel to secure a good 12 to 15 hours a day for transcribing and writing. I woke up at six, started working half an hour later and generally finished around midnight. I'd take a break midday and spend time with my daughter. Except for that, I concentrated on these pages.

When housekeeping knocked on the door, I asked them to replace the towels in the bathroom and make the bed. A quick five-minute task. I did not want to be interrupted when the words and thoughts were flowing.

As I was checking out on the last day, one of the maids stopped me in the hall.

"Are you writing a thesis?" she asked.

"Not a thesis, a book," I said.

"I have to admit," she divulged, "I cheated a little bit and read your introduction."

She seemed relieved I wasn't angry. Then she continued.

"I swear," she said, "Steven Tyler was in my closet when he wrote 'Amazing.' I couldn't believe it the first time I heard it. I was driving down the road and I started to cry. I pulled over and just started crying."

This is the magic of recovery, the warmth of the fellowship.

One of the saddest things I see is someone caught in the grips of alcoholism, especially when all I can do is observe from the sidelines. I've worked with several people who have an alcohol problem. They knew I was sober and they didn't want help. I would lob some subtle hints at them in case they wanted to talk, but to their way of thinking their lives were fine. My career was soaring while theirs was at a standstill. In their eyes, I was the odd one because I kept working hard, I kept achieving. They were stuck in mediocrity, and happy in that situation. Their behavior was acceptable to them. What can you do other than be there for those people if and when they need you?

In 1995, one of the world's most brilliant artists, dancer Alexander Godunov, died from the "cumulative effects of acute alcoholism," according to his spokesman. Here's a guy who had achieved every bit of success he'd strived for. Still, the disease grabbed him, talked to him, convinced him not to leave, then killed him. It's an inside job. External fixes just don't work.

Alcoholism and drug abuse claim lives, crush endless relationships and dispense a toxic example to our children.

If there is one common thread that weaves through this book, it's leaving you with the message that it doesn't have to get any worse. The pain and suffering can end—right now. If you're recovering now, it can and will get better, brighter and stronger, even if you're on top of the sober mountain already. That mountain will continue to rise with a powerful program. I will never forget Steven Tyler's face when he looked me square in the eyes, his so clear and filled with emotion, mine still hanging onto blame, shame and fright. That was my first miracle of sobriety.

Continue to work your program, to ask questions, to seek out the answers to your heart. Keep in mind that times will be tough on occasions, but remember: we are fortunate enough to hold the tools to climb to great heights. We now know how to handle fear, shame, manipulation and intolerance. We have been given faith, honesty, forgiveness, tolerance, understanding, and, most of all, we have love. We now know how to love and how to be loved. We are at peace.

If you're like me, you'll go back and read certain interviews over and over. I pick up some little piece of information that makes me stronger each and every time I reread the book. Know that there are tools for a successful recovery and the foundation for love, if that urge ever enters your mind. If those negative inner voices start to talk to you, remember: these people have shared their stories for you, for no one else but you.